The Nomad's Guide to Cooking on the Road

The Nomad's Guide to Cooking on the Road

Easy, budget-friendly dishes to cook while travelling in your RV or van or at the camping or caravan site

David Cowie

NEW HOLLAND

Contents

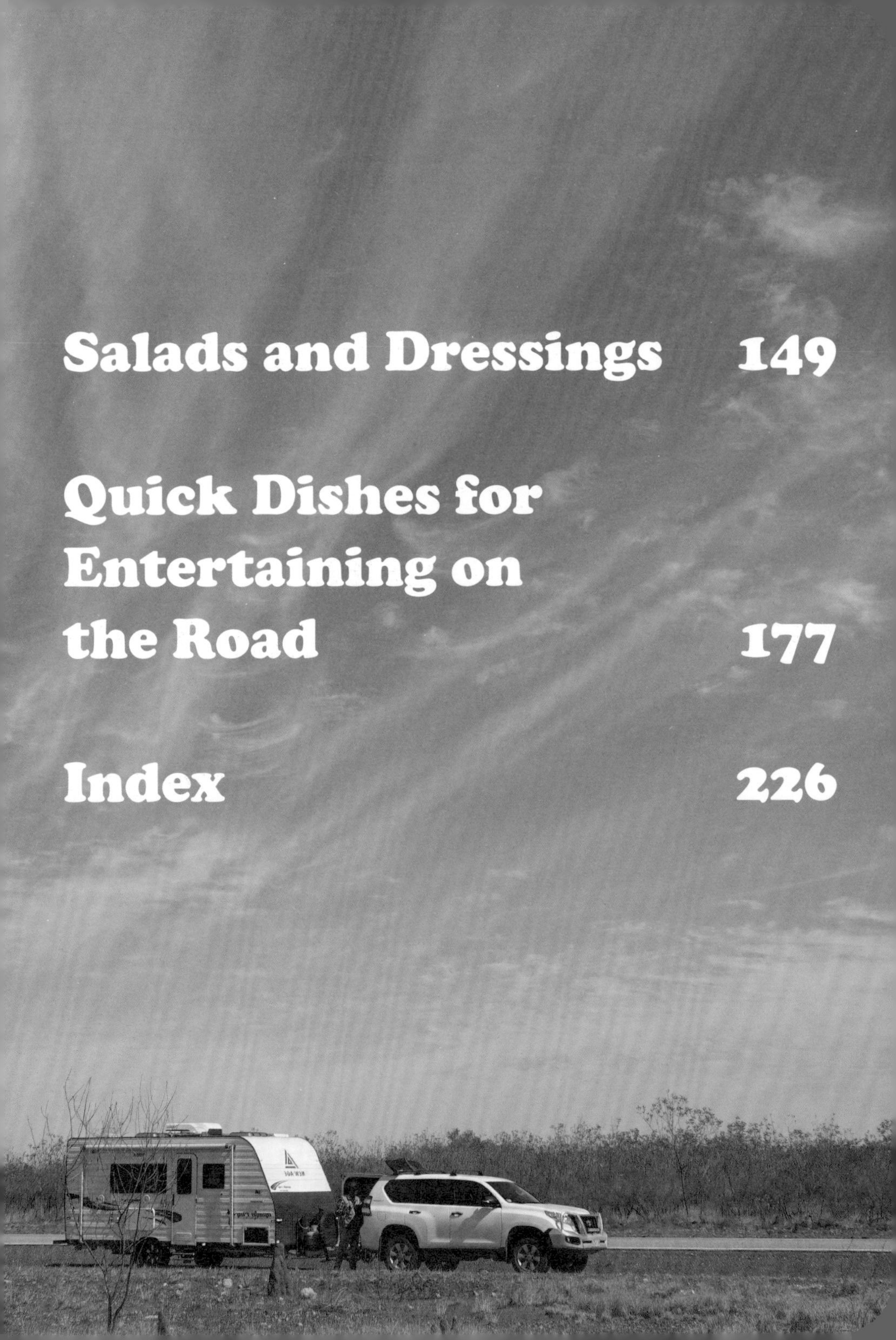

Introduction

Cooking on the road is about using the method you have available where you are that day, and taking advantage of 240-volt power when it is available, as most electrical appliances will draw too much power from your battery banks.

You can use a gas black stone (flat plate) BBQ, charcoal grill, camp oven, van/RV convection microwave oven, pie maker, air fryer, sandwich press/jaffle maker, toaster or multi-cooker. Most of the recipes can be made using any of these methods.

Multi-use equipment is a great addition to your kitchen. A small bullet-type blender can be used to make smoothies, dice veggies, blend sauces, grind coffee beans and even make frozen margaritas. And the multi-cooker – a combination of slow cooker, pressure cooker, rice cooker and air fryer – can grill, bake, steam, slow/pressure cook, steam and dehydrate, taking up much less space than all those individual items.

While on the road you want to take advantage of the times when you have power, which is not limited to when you are at a powered site. You could use a slow cooker for baking or meals with longer cooking times; prepare and cook a frittata for eating the next day on the road; or cook meals in advance and freeze or store in the fridge.

Alternatively, if you have above-average fire-making and maintaining skills you can cook anywhere that you can get your hands on firewood, as long as you're not using an open fire at a time or place where there's an extreme fire danger.

It is helpful to plan meals that have similar ingredients or use the leftovers of a meal as a base or side dish for another meal. Knowing what you are going to cook each day helps reduce the cost and amount of food you are picking up on each shopping trip and leaves room for the essentials – like beer and wine!

Food Storage and Preservation

Not all vehicles have sufficient refrigeration or freezer space, and those that do will require electricity to run them, which might not always be available. When you consider the space limitations that you'll have to deal with as a nomad you need to rethink the way that you do food.

You will have more time to enjoy yourself and need to buy and store fewer ingredients if you can stick to meals that are simple to prepare. This is where a slow cooker comes in. The great advantage of slow cooking is that you can buy cheaper but tougher cuts of meats that are more flavoursome and lend themselves to long, slow cooking to bring their flavours out and tenderise them until they melt in your mouth. Slow cooking is also easy. You can just bung in a whole bunch of ingredients in the morning, set and forget, and by evening your meals are ready. Of course, you need a steady supply of power to make this work, but that's what trailer parks and/or solar electricity are for. Slow cooked meals also freeze really easily, so leftovers become the gift that just keeps on giving.

Some other things to consider include:

- Dried ingredients, such as nuts, dried fruit and grains are high-density, lightweight foods that you can graze on.
- Storing dry foods in containers that can be stacked makes them last longer as well as being easier to store in cupboards.
- Leafy vegetables, like Chinese greens and spinach, as well as cauliflower and broccoli, don't store well, so consume them as soon as possible.
- Root vegetables and squashes like pumpkin store for a long time especially in cold conditions, but 'a long time' doesn't mean 'forever' so don't wait until they start sprouting before you eat them.
- Cans are wonderful for wet foods, but they are heavy, so where possible consider buying food that is packaged in Tetra Paks.

- You might be amazed at what you can accomplish with limited equipment. Clever cooks just love sharing their cleverness with other people and if you just ask around, you'll get some great tips. You'll also find plenty of great videos online to get you inspired.
- If you're in a town for a while and have friends or contacts with access to a kitchen, it pays to make up a whole bunch of meals like curries, soups, stews and the like that can be frozen and reheated in a microwave later.

Cooking equipment essentials

✔ BBQ of your liking. Gas is easier and there's nothing like a flame to cook a steak!

✔ Moka pot or Aeropress coffee maker (essential if you can't do without a good morning coffee!)

✔ Cast iron fry pan with a lid (can be used on open flames)

✔ Large saucepan with lid (as many as you like/can fit)

✔ Baking tray/aluminium trays

✔ Colander/strainer

✔ Can opener

✔ Corkscrew/bottle opener (waiters friend)

✔ Sharp knives

✔ Cutting board

✔ Metal tongs

✔ Large spoon

✔ Wooden spoons

✔ Spatula/fish slice, whisk, masher

✔ Peeler

✔ Grater

✔ Flat metal skewers

✔ Bamboo skewers or BBQ skewers

✔ Egg rings – silicone would be ideal

✔ Mixing bowls (can also be used as a salad serving bowl)

✔ Measuring cups/spoons

✔ Aluminium foil

✔ Cling wrap

✔ Baking paper

✔ Sealable containers for dry foods (like rice, flour, pasta)

✔ Large storage containers for bulk storage of food

- ✔ Microwave-proof containers
- ✔ Plates and bowls
- ✔ Drinking glasses
- ✔ Coffee and tea cups
- ✔ Napkins/paper towel
- ✔ Scissors
- ✔ Tea towel
- ✔ Zip-lock bags
- ✔ Garbage bags
- ✔ Hand wash/sanitiser
- ✔ Dish washing soap

Pantry Essentials

- ✔ Salt and pepper
- ✔ Assorted spices (chilli flakes, basil, rosemary, garlic powder, onion powder, oregano, Italian seasoning, parsley, cumin and paprika to name a few, but you might like others)
- ✔ BBQ rubs (so many, so little space ha-ha)
- ✔ Sugar
- ✔ Flour
- ✔ Baking powder
- ✔ Yeast
- ✔ Stock powder or cubes (chicken, beef or veg, up to you)
- ✔ Cereal: oats/muesli/Weet-Bix
- ✔ Bread crumbs
- ✔ Rice
- ✔ Dried pasta
- ✔ Popcorn
- ✔ Canned vegetables (tomatoes, chick peas, beans, baked beans etc.)
- ✔ Canned tuna
- ✔ Tinned and packet soup
- ✔ Oil (olive and vegetable for frying)
- ✔ Vinegar
- ✔ Tomato sauce
- ✔ BBQ sauce
- ✔ Mayonnaise
- ✔ Mustard
- ✔ Pickles
- ✔ Soy sauce
- ✔ Hot sauce
- ✔ Salad dressing
- ✔ Worcestershire sauce
- ✔ Tea and coffee
- ✔ Long-life milk
- ✔ Your favourite spreads: honey, jam, peanut butter, Vegemite
- ✔ Trail mix, nuts
- ✔ Instant noodles

This is not the be all and end all list of pantry essentials. I am sure that you will have favourites you want to add to this short list or other items you would leave behind.

Kitchen Management on the Road

There are many small time-saving tricks. The idea is to work out how to effectively use your time in the kitchen, and enjoy the tasks at hand. Keep an eye on the way you use the limited benches or space in your kitchen and even think about using a space outside. When cooking in confined or limited spaces, get in the habit of tidying and cleaning as you cook, then the kitchen will be as tidy once you've finished a simple recipe as when you started!

Consider how much walking you do backwards and forwards to the sink, the stove and the refrigerator. Little things add up, and making some small changes can save a great deal of time you could instead be enjoying on the road. Try to have your cutting board next to the cooking pot or frying pan, making it quick and easy to swipe all of the cut food off the cutting board and into a pot without even turning around. And having your dried herbs and spices within reach will be a time saver as well.

When you're out shopping, it's worth keeping an eye on the different time-saving foods available. Fresh lasagne sheets, quick-cook polenta and fast-cooking brown rice to name a few. Keep an eye out for new products, as there are always innovations in the range of quick foods, which can be a great way of saving cooking time.

While pre-prepared salad mixes appear fast, unless you're off camping with limited equipment, it's better to cut and combine salad leaves yourself, as a whole lettuce will go a long way. Most foods that are pre-cut cost more, do not last as long and have lost valuable nutrients and flavour by the time they reach the supermarket, the fridge, and finally your salad bowl. Fast is good, but fresh is always best. Pre-prepared salads do redeem themselves if you are going to use them that day or if you are preparing a meal for a large group.

Try to plan your meals for the road a day in advance, as you may be able to do the preparation for two recipes at one time, making the second meal much easier than the first. Look for meals that you are able to use the leftovers to make a second meal, or can add to and extend for the next day's lunch or dinner.

To save time later, pre-cut and freeze foods such as meats for stews and casseroles. You can also chop and freeze things like onions, chilli and ginger and if you regularly use them together you can even keep them in the same freezer bag.

Remember that if you're roasting, a couple of dishes can be placed into the oven at one time – choose a second dish that can be baked alongside your dinner, a dish that will reheat the following night. That way you get two meals from one cooking time.

Starches and heavy foods take the longest to cook, so if you're using your oven remember to always preheat it to the desired temperature and use smaller cuts of larger, dense foods like meat and potatoes. Use smaller cuts of meat and butterfly larger cuts of meat if roasting. Also consider what you can cook on the BBQ, such as whole deboned chicken and lamb legs.

Breakfast

Banana Smoothie

Makes 1

Ingredients

½ cup milk
½ banana
juice of 1 orange

½ cup natural (plain) yoghurt
2 teaspoons apple juice
concentrate

Place all the ingredients in a blender with four ice cubes and blend until smooth.

Banana and Honey Smoothie

Makes 2

Ingredients

2 large ripe bananas
1 cup milk
⅔ cup honey yoghurt

4 tablespoons mixed and
ground linseeds, sunflower
seeds and almond meal
(ground almonds)

Cut the bananas into pieces and place in a food processor or blender. Add the milk, yoghurt and ground nuts and seeds. Blend until smooth and thick.

Pour the smoothie into two large glasses to serve.

Porridge

Serves 2

Ingredients

¾ cup rolled oats
2 cups water

2 tablespoons brown sugar
⅔ cup cold milk, to serve

Place the oats and 1½ cups of the water in a bowl. Cover and soak at room temperature overnight. The oats will expand so make sure there is room in the bowl.

Transfer the oats and liquid to a medium saucepan. Add the remaining water and bring to the boil. Reduce the heat and simmer, stirring, for a few minutes or until the liquid has been absorbed. Divide the porridge between serving bowls.

Sprinkle with brown sugar and serve with cold milk.

Bircher Muesli

Serves 2

Ingredients

1¼ cups rolled oats
1 cup apple juice

1 apple, grated
½ cup natural (plain) yoghurt

Place the oats and apple juice in a bowl. Cover and set aside for 2 hours or overnight in the refrigerator.

When ready to eat, stir through the grated apple and yoghurt and divide between two serving bowls.

French Toast

Makes 2 pieces of toast

Ingredients

1 egg

¼ cup milk

2 slices bread

2 tablespoons butter

For Savoury Toast

salt and freshly
    ground black pepper

For Sweet Toast

1 tablespoon sugar

1 teaspoon vanilla extract

½ teaspoon ground cinnamon

Whisk together the egg and milk.

For savoury toast, add salt and pepper to the mixture and whisk well.

For sweet toast, add sugar, vanilla extract and cinnamon to the mixture and whisk well.

Melt the butter in a frying pan over medium heat. Dip the bread slices in the egg mixture, covering both sides. Place in the heated pan and fry for a few minutes on each side.

Serve with bacon and eggs or fresh fruit.

Sweet Corn Pancakes

Serves 4

Ingredients

¼ cup milk

1 tablespoon butter, melted,
plus extra for frying

100 g canned creamed corn

1 teaspoon chopped fresh or
dried chives

1 egg

45 g self-raising flour

salt and pepper

bacon and tomatoes, to serve

Combine the milk, melted butter, creamed corn, chives and egg in a bowl and season with salt and pepper. Add the flour and stir until smooth.

Heat a little butter in a frying pan. Pour in a small ladle of batter and fry over low heat for 2 minutes on each side, or until puffed and golden.

Serve with fried bacon and tomatoes or whatever you have available.

Note: The pancakes are also great with avocado and poached eggs.

Pikelets

Makes about 20

Ingredients

115 g self-raising flour
pinch of salt
2 tablespoons sugar
1 egg
1 cup milk

2 tablespoons butter
1 teaspoon golden syrup
a little oil or butter, for greasing
butter, jam and cream, to serve

Sift the flour and salt into a bowl and add the sugar. In another bowl, beat the egg and milk together then stir into the flour.

Melt the butter and golden syrup together in a pan over a low heat, stirring until melted, then add to the flour and egg mixture.

Brush a griddle or frying pan with a little oil or butter and when it is hot, drop in the batter in spoonfuls (about a tablespoon), leaving room to spread. Cook over a medium heat until the underside is browned and small bubbles appear on the surface, then flip and fry the other side until cooked.

Serve warm with butter or cold with jam and whipped cream or sliced bananas.

Note: Makes a good snack to go with a cup of tea. Pikelets are also delicious served with sliced banana.

Banana Bread

Serves 8

115 g butter, softened
200 g superfine (caster) sugar
2 eggs, lightly beaten
3 ripe bananas, peeled
2 tablespoons honey
2 tablespoons lemon juice

1 teaspoon vanilla extract
175 g self-raising flour, sifted
½ teaspoon baking soda
1 teaspoon ground cinnamon
60 g almond meal
  (ground almonds)

Preheat the oven to 180°C. Lightly grease a 23 x 15 cm loaf tin, a muffin tray, or two small loaf tins if you are using an air fryer.

In a mixing bowl, beat the butter and sugar with and whisk until light and creamy (or if you have access to one you can use a stand mixer). Add the eggs and mix until combined.

In a separate bowl Combine the bananas, honey, lemon juice and vanilla. Mash until smooth.

Add the banana mixture to the butter and sugar mixture and mix until well combined. Gently fold in the flour, baking soda, cinnamon and almond meal.

Pour the batter into the prepared tin and bake for 50–60 minutes, or until cooked through and a skewer comes out clean. Muffins will take 20–30 minutes to cook.

Leave to cool for 5 minutes then turn out onto a wire rack. Slice and serve with butter. Even better when toasted later on.

Note: You can make this in an air fryer (160°C) and you can use most dishes or pans that are ovenproof – glass, ceramic, metal or silicone – as long as it fits into your air fryer. In the air fryer it should only take 30 minutes but read your settings menu for an indication of how long your air fryer will take.

Peanut Butter Muffins

Makes 12

Ingredients

175 g plain (all-purpose) flour
45 g sugar
1 tablespoon baking powder
½ teaspoon salt
100 g rolled oats

250 ml milk
1 egg
115 g smooth peanut butter
¼ cup oil

Preheat the oven to 200°C.

Line a muffin tray with paper cases or lightly grease.

Combine the flour, sugar, baking powder and salt in a large bowl. Stir to combine then make a well in the centre.

Place the oats and milk in a medium-sized bowl. Add the egg and peanut butter to the oat mixture and beat well.

Add the oil and stir through. Add the oat mix to the flour mix, stirring just enough to combine. Three-quarters fill the paper cases, then bake for 15–20 minutes, or until golden and cooked through. Serve warm.

Note: These can be made in an air fryer (160°C) and will take around 12–15 minutes to cook but check the instruction manual of your machine.

Bacon and Avocado Muffins

Serves 2

Ingredients

4 rashers bacon, halved and rind removed

2 English muffins, halved

2 tablespoons mayonnaise

1 ripe avocado, halved and pit removed

salt and pepper

Preheat a non-stick frying pan on medium-high heat. Cook the bacon to your liking.

Toast the muffins in a toaster until golden brown. Spread mayonnaise on the muffin tops.

Slice the avocado and arrange on the base of the muffins. Season to taste. Top with bacon and cover with muffin tops.

Smoked Salmon Bagel

Serves 2

Ingredients

2 bagels, halved
4 tablespoons crème fraîche
2 slices smoked salmon

baby rocket (arugula) leaves
or iceberg lettuce

Toast the bagels until golden brown. Spread crème fraîche on both halves. Arrange smoked salmon slices on the bottom halves and top with rocket. Place the bagel lids on top and serve.

Note: If you can't get crème fraîche you can use cream cheese.

Bacon & Egg Pies

Makes 12

12 small soft tacos (tortillas)
500 g bacon, diced
1 1/2 cups sour cream

1/4 cup parsley, chopped
12 eggs
oil, for greasing

Preheat the oven to 200°C.

Lightly grease a 12-cup jumbo muffin tray and place a taco into each muffin cup.

Fry the bacon in a frying pan for 3–4 minutes or until lightly golden. Drain on absorbent paper and cool for 5 minutes. Divide three-quarters of the bacon evenly between the tacos.

In a bowl, whisk the sour cream and parsley together until well combined, then pour over the bacon. Crack an egg on top of each pie then top with the remaining bacon.

Bake for 25–30 minutes, or until the taco is golden and the filling is cooked. Leave to set for 5 minutes before removing from the muffin tray. Serve hot or cold.

Note: If the tacos are a little hard to form in the muffin tray you may need to microwave them for 10–15 seconds to soften.

These are great on-the-road snacks so make up a batch before you hit the road for the day.

Breakfast Wrap

Serves 4

Ingredients

8 eggs
salt and freshly
   ground black pepper
4 rashers bacon, diced
30 g butter

1 medium tomato, seeds
   removed then diced
⅔ cup milk
4 flour tortillas
100 g grated cheddar cheese
   (most cheeses will do)

Crack the eggs into a bowl, add the milk and salt and pepper to taste, whisk then set aside.

Place the bacon in a well-oiled fry pan on medium heat and fry until almost cooked then remove from the pan and set aside.

Add the butter to the pan, making sure it is not too hot as you don't want to burn the butter. When the butter is melted pour the eggs into the fry pan and start to move them around so they become scrambled. Add the tomatoes and bacon. Continue to cook until everything is well combined and the eggs are cooked then set aside.

Warm the tortillas, evenly divide the egg mixture between them, then top with the cheese and fold.

Grill briefly on each side to ensure the cheese is melted.

Note: Add hot sauce for a bit of spice or baby spinach if you have it on hand. You could also serve the eggs on toast.

These can be wrapped in aluminium foil then frozen. Reheat on the BBQ plate, sandwich press or in the air fryer.

Pancakes

Makes 10

Ingredients

⅔ cup self-raising flour

2 tablespoons sugar

1 egg

⅔ cup milk

30 g butter

maple syrup, to serve

Sift the flour into a large mixing bowl. Add the sugar and stir to combine.

In another bowl, whisk the egg and milk together.

Make a well in the centre of the flour mixture. Pour in the egg mixture and beat with a wooden spoon until smooth.

Place a little butter in a frying pan. Heat over a medium-high heat until melted and sizzling.

Pour 3–4 tablespoons of batter into the frying pan. Cook until bubbles form on top of the pancake. Turn over and cook for another minute or two.

Place the cooked pancake on a plate and repeat with the remaining pancake batter.

Stack three or four pancakes on each serving plate. Serve with a drizzle of maple syrup.

Toad in a Hole (Egg Toast)

Serves 2

Ingredients

2 eggs

2 slices of bread

butter or oil spray

salt and pepper to taste

Make a hole in the middle of each slice of bread using a small glass or cup to cut out a circle.

Oil or grease a frying pan and heat on medium. Put a slice of bread in the frying pan for a few minutes or until brown and then flip over. Crack an egg into the hole and continue to cook.

You could put the egg in at the beginning if you feel confident enough to flip the egg over to cook the other side.

When the eggs are cooked to how your like them and the toast is cooked through serve with salt and pepper to taste or your favourite sauce. You could also add chilli flakes, parsley or whatever herbs you have available.

Easy Meals

Lamb Rissoles

Serves 6

Ingredients

500 g lamb mince
1 small onion, finely diced
½ cup breadcrumbs
¼ cup diced
    chargrilled capsicum (bell
    pepper)
1 egg
1 clove garlic, finely chopped
1 teaspoon ground cumin
¼ bunch fresh mint, finely
    chopped (keep some for
    garnish)
spray oil for cooking

Place all the ingredients in a bowl and mix well to combine. Season with salt and pepper.

Divide mince mixture into 6 portions then shape each portion into a patty.

Heat BBQ plate or chargrill over medium–low heat.
Spray both sides of the rissoles with oil. Cook, turning occasionally, for 12 to 15 minutes or until cooked through.

Serve on a platter or make a burger.

Grilled Prawns

Serves 4

Ingredients
1 kg green prawns,
    peeled and de-veined

Marinade
1 cup olive oil

¼ cup lemon juice

¼ cup finely chopped onion

2 cloves garlic, crushed

parsley, finely chopped

To make the marinade, place all marinade ingredients in a large bowl and mix well. Add the prawns to the bowl and combine. Cover and let stand for several hours in the refrigerator. Drain the prawns.

Place the prawns in a heavy-based frying pan or skillet and cook over medium heat on a BBQ or cooktop for 10–15 minutes, or until pink and cooked through. Stir frequently and add a little marinade while cooking.

Serve immediately.

Hamburgers

Serves 6

Ingredients

1 small onion, grated
500 g minced steak
3 tablespoons plain flour
¼ cup milk

125 g extra plain flour
¼ cup oil
6 hamburger buns
tomato sauce

Mix onion and meat thoroughly in a bowl using a wooden spoon.

Add flour and mix in thoroughly. Pour milk over meat mixture and stir in well.

Place extra flour in a small bowl. Make a heaped tablespoon of the meat mixture into a ball and roll it in the flour until it is well coated. Transfer to a plate and flatten slightly. Continue until all the meat is used.

Pour oil into a frying pan and place over a medium heat. (They can also be grilled or barbecued.) When the oil starts to bubble, gently place hamburger patties in the pan. Cook until the bottom of the hamburgers are brown, then flip them over and cook until they are brown on the other side.

Drain the patties on absorbent paper.

Place patties on hamburger buns and add tomato sauce.

Variations: Add sliced cheese, sliced cucumber, sliced tomatoes, sliced beetroot and lettuce – or salad ingredients of your choice.

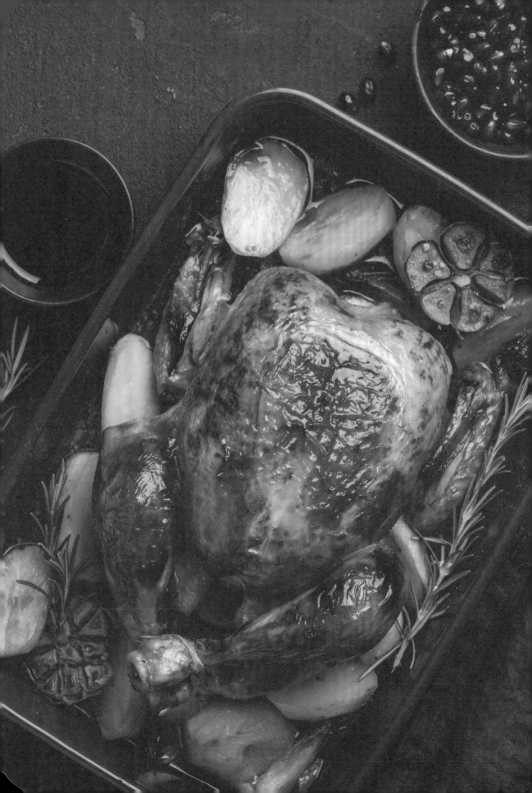

Roast Chicken

Serves 4–6

Ingredients

1 x 1.5 kg chicken, washed
and dried
salt and freshly ground
black pepper, to taste

3 tablespoons olive oil
1 cup chicken stock

Preheat oven to 180°C.

Rub chicken with salt, pepper and half the olive oil.

Truss chicken and place in a greased roasting pan with remaining oil. Cook in the oven, basting occasionally, for 1 hour, or until tender and golden brown all over. Remove chicken and keep warm.

While chicken is cooking heat the chicken stock. Add the stock to the pan juices and bring to the boil. Strain into a sauce boat and serve with the chicken, roast potatoes and green vegetables.

You can also cook the chicken in the air fryer, which will take 30 minutes to cook on the chicken setting (or up to 180°C).

Mussels Marinières

Serves 4

Ingredients

1 kg mussels
2 tablespoons butter
1 small onion, thinly sliced
1 clove garlic, chopped

¼ cup white wine
freshly ground black pepper
¼ cup chopped parsley

Rinse mussels under cool running water, scrubbing the outside. De-beard the mussels if necessary by pulling the fibrous beard towards the hinge of the shell to remove.

In a large saucepan heat the butter over medium-high heat. This can also be done on the BBQ grill if you don't have access to a cooktop.

When the butter starts to foam, add the onion and garlic. Stir and cook until the onions are transparent and garlic is soft, about 2–3 minutes. Add the wine and stir to combine.

Add the cleaned mussels to the pot, cover, and steam for 2–3 minutes until the mussels have just opened. Discard any mussels which remain closed.

Transfer to serving dishes and pour over the liquid, or leave in the pan to serve. Season with pepper to taste and garnish with parsley. Serve with crusty bread.

Note: You can buy mussels ready to cook, scrubbed and de-bearded, from most supermarkets.

Spicy Barbecued Baby Octopus

Serves 4–6

Ingredients

1 kg baby octopus
½ bottle red wine
⅓ cup balsamic vinegar
1 garlic clove, crushed
¼ cup soy sauce
¼ cup hot sauce

¼ cup barbecue sauce
¼ cup tomato sauce
salt and pepper, to taste
20 g chopped coriander
(cilantro), to garnish
1 lemon, cut into wedges

Place the octopus, red wine and balsamic vinegar in a saucepan and bring to the boil over medium heat. Reduce to a simmer for 15 minutes.

Drain the octopus, then place in a large bowl. Combine the garlic, soy sauce, hot sauce, tomato sauce and barbecue sauce. Add to the octopus and mix to ensure the octopus is well coated.

Cook the octopus on a hot BBQ grill, while basting with the sauce, for about 5 minutes or until charred. Do not overcook or the octopus will be chewy.

When cooked, place on a serving plate with lemon and garnish with coriander.

Korean Barbecue Beef Ribs

Serves 4–6

Ingredients
12 beef ribs, 7 cm long

Marinade
1 cup soy sauce

45 g sesame seeds, toasted

3 teaspoons sugar

1 teaspoon chilli

3 large cloves garlic, crushed

Place the ribs in a large plastic bag. Combine the soy sauce, sesame seeds, sugar, chilli and garlic, mix well then pour over the ribs. Press the air out of the bag and seal the top securely.

Refrigerate for 4 hours, turning the bag over occasionally.

Remove the ribs and BBQ (10 cm above the hot coals if using charcoal) for about 15 minutes, or until the ribs are brown and crisp. Turn the ribs over occasionally.

Steak and Blue Cheese on Turkish Bread

Serves 4

Ingredients

500 g thin steak
salt and freshly ground pepper,
   to taste
4 Turkish buns, ciabatta, or any
   choice of bread or bun

¼ cup mayonnaise
coleslaw
200 g blue cheese, crumbed

Preheat the BBQ grill plate to high heat.

Season the steak with salt and pepper on both sides. Place the steak on the grill and cook to your liking. Remove the steak from the grill and rest it while toasting the bread on the grill.

Slice the steak across the grain. Butter one side of the toasted bread with mayonnaise. Top with coleslaw, then the sliced steak and some crumbled blue cheese. Top with the other slice of bread. Serve immediately.

Quick Sesame Chicken Wings

Serves 4–6

Ingredients

2 kg chicken wings, tips removed
½ cup honey
¼ cup light soy sauce
3 tablespoons sherry
½ teaspoon fresh ginger, minced

½ teaspoon fresh garlic, minced
¼ cup sesame seeds, toasted
1 long green shallot (scallion),
    finely sliced, to serve

Combine the honey, soy sauce, sherry, ginger and garlic. Stir together to make a marinade.

Place the wings in a large container. Cover with marinade and place in the refrigerator for 1 hour.

Place half the wings in a microwave-safe dish and microwave for 7 minutes on high. Remove and microwave the remainder.

Heat the BBQ until hot. Place a wire cake rack over the grill bars and place the wings on the rack. Brush with any marinade left in the bowl. Turn and brush the wings frequently for 6 minutes until brown and crisp.

While the wings are crisping, spread the sesame seeds on a foil tray and place on the BBQ. Shake occasionally as they toast.

Sprinkle sesame seeds and spring onion over the chicken wings and serve.

Barbecued Chicken and Avocado Quesadilla

Serves 4

Ingredients

2 chicken breasts
barbecue rub of your choice
    (optional)
1 red onion, finely sliced
1 garlic clove, finely sliced

1 avocado, cut into long,
    thin slices
100 g cheddar cheese
100 g provolone cheese
8 flour tortillas

Rub the chicken with the barbecue rub until coated evenly and leave to stand for 30 minutes.

Lightly fry the onion and garlic on an oiled BBQ flat plate until golden. Remove and set aside until needed.

Add the lightly oiled chicken fillet and grill for 4–5 minutes per side (depending on thickness of the fillets), or until cooked through.

Remove the chicken from the BBQ, place on a cutting board and cut into 1 cm slices.

Divide the chicken, avocado, onion, garlic and cheeses between the flour tortillas. Cover with a tortilla.

Place on the BBQ flat plate until lightly toasted on both sides and the cheese is melted. Cut and serve warm.

There is a recipe for barbecue rub on page 71.

Thai Grilled Chicken

Serves 4–6

Ingredients

2 cloves garlic, crushed
1½ teaspoons ground coriander
2 teaspoons turmeric
salt and freshly ground
    black pepper

2 tablespoons oil
500 g chicken wings
coriander (cilantro),
    chopped to garnish
sweet chilli sauce

Mix the garlic, ground coriander, turmeric, salt, pepper and oil together. Rub over the chicken. Set aside for at least 30 minutes, or cover and refrigerate overnight for a minimum of 4 hours if you can.

Heat a grill or BBQ. Grill the marinated chicken pieces until the juices run clear when tested.

Serve garnished with chopped coriander and sweet chilli sauce.

Note: Can also be done in an air fryer or in the oven.

Sticky Chicken Drumettes

Serves 4–6

Ingredients

1 kg chicken drumettes
¼ cup soy sauce
¼ cup barbecue sauce
¼ cup honey

1 garlic clove, crushed
1 teaspoon salt
½ teaspoon ground pepper

Place the drumettes in a large zip-lock bag. Add the remaining ingredients and shake the bag to coat the drumettes. Refrigerate until needed.

Preheat the BBQ grill to medium-high heat.

Cook the drumettes for 15–20 minutes, or until golden brown, crispy and completely cooked through.

Keep basting the chicken with the marinade throughout the cooking process. If the drumettes begin to burn, move them to a cooler part of the grill or reduce the heat.

Remove from the BBQ and place on a platter to serve.

The chicken can also be cooked in an air fryer for 30 minutes or in an oven for 1 hour on 180°C.

Butterflied Lemon Chicken

Serves 2–4

Ingredients

1.2–1.5 kg whole chicken,
   cut through the backbone
3 tablespoons Worcestershire
   sauce
salt

$\frac{1}{2}$ teaspoon cracked
   black pepper
1 garlic clove, crushed
juice and zest of 1 lemon
olive oil

Put the chicken on a chopping board, breast side down, and using a pair of kitchen scissors, cut through each side of the backbone.

Turn the chicken breast side up and open the chicken. Place your hand on top and flatten. Rub the chicken with the Worcestershire sauce, salt, pepper, garlic, lemon and olive oil. Cover the chicken and let marinate in the fridge for at least 1 hour and up to 8 hours.

Preheat the BBQ grill to medium-high heat. Place the chicken on the grill, breast side down, and cook for 15–20 minutes, depending on size. Turn and cook for a further 15–20 minutes.

Cook until the chicken is just cooked through then rest, covered, for 5 minutes before serving.

Sticky Beer Can Chicken

Serves 6

Ingredients

1 large whole chicken
1 teaspoon vegetable oil
½ teaspoon sea salt
¼ teaspoon pepper

½ teaspoon chicken spice rub
1 can beer (or soda can may
   also be used)
3 tablespoons barbecue sauce

Pat down the chicken with a paper towel to absorb any moisture. Rub the chicken inside and out with vegetable oil. Season with salt, pepper and spice rub.

Open the beer can and pour out half of the liquid. Place the can on a cutting board and lower the chicken onto the can so it looks like it is sitting on it. Position the legs like a tripod so the chicken sits upright.

Prepare the BBQ for indirect cooking on medium heat. Place the chicken in the middle of the BBQ and close the lid. Cook the chicken for about an hour or until golden brown.

The chicken is done when the juices run clear when a skewer is pushed into the thickest part of the thigh. Brush the chicken with barbecue sauce and cook for a further 10 minutes until dark and sticky.

Filet Mignon

Serves 4

Ingredients

4 bacon rashers, rind removed

4 slices of fillet steak,
  3.5 cm thick

salt and freshly ground
  black pepper, to taste

parsley butter

Wrap a bacon rasher around each fillet and secure with toothpicks.

Preheat grill to hot and brush rack with oil. Place fillet under grill rack, 8 cm below heat.

Grill for 3–4 minutes on each side for rare steak, 2 minutes longer on each side for medium rare steak. Turn fillets gently so you don't pierce the meat and let the juices escape.

Season with salt and pepper, garnish with parsley butter and serve immediately with roast potatoes.

Steak Sandwich

Serves 4

Ingredients

500 g rump or sirloin steak (whichever you prefer)

salt and freshly ground pepper

Sandwich

4 sourdough or other long rolls
mayonnaise, to serve
rocket (arugula)

2 tomatoes, sliced
caramelised onion, to serve

Prepare a BBQ for direct heat cooking on high heat (or you can use a frying pan on the cooktop).

Season the steak with salt and pepper on both sides then place the steak on the grill or in the frying pan and cook to your liking.

Rest the steak while you toast the rolls on the grill.

Slice the steak then butter one side of the toasted rolls. Add the mayonnaise, rocket and tomato then season with salt and pepper to taste and top with the sliced steak and caramelised onion.

Roast Beef with Caramelised Onions

Serves 2–4

Ingredients

2 tablespoons olive oil
2 medium onions,
   halved and thinly sliced
1½ tablespoons balsamic
   vinegar
1 tablespoon brown sugar
1½ tablespoons thyme leaves

1 French bread stick or baguette,
   cut into 1½ cm slices
olive oil spray
⅓ cup light cream cheese
14 large thin slices of rare roast
   beef, cut in half

Preheat oven to 220°C. Heat oil in a saucepan over low heat. Cook onion for 10 minutes, or until soft, stirring from time to time. Add balsamic vinegar and brown sugar. Cover and cook for a further 15 minutes, or until caramelised, stirring from time to time. Transfer onions to a bowl and stir in thyme leaves.

Meanwhile, place bread slices on a baking tray and spray with olive oil. Place in the oven and cook for 5–6 minutes or until just golden.

Spread bread evenly with cream cheese. Top with roast beef and caramelised onions.

Veggie Pita Pocket

Serves 2

Ingredients

2 pita pockets

3 tablespoons hummus

1 medium carrot, grated

2 tablespoon cheddar cheese,
  grated

1 small cooked beetroot, grated

20 g lettuce leaves, shredded

1 teaspoon lemon juice

Cut the pita pocket in half and spread each half with the hummus.

Mix the remaining ingredients in a bowl. Divide the mixture between each pocket.

Barbecue Rub

Ingredients

60 g brown sugar

2 teaspoons paprika

1 teaspoon salt

1 teaspoon mustard powder

1 teaspoon black pepper

1 teaspoon chilli flakes

1 teaspoon onion powder

1 teaspoon garlic powder

Combine all of the ingredients.

Notes: Store in an airtight container for up to 6 months. You can increase the amount of pepper and mustard to make the mix hot and spicy.

Potato Skins with Toppings

Makes 4 pieces per potato

Ingredients
4 baking potatoes

Bacon and Mushroom Topping
2 rashers bacon,
    chopped and sautéed
4 button mushrooms,
    sliced and sautéed
1 tablespoon parsley, chopped

Prawn and Chive Topping
2 tablespoons sour cream
2 tablespoons chives, chopped
¾ cup prawns, cooked and
    chopped
salt and pepper to taste

Chicken and Peanut Topping
¾ cup cooked chicken, diced
1 tablespoon toasted pine nuts
3 tablespoons long green shallots
    (scallions), chopped
2 tablespoons sour cream
freshly ground black pepper

Preheat the oven to 180°C. Wash and dry each potato. Pierce with a fork and place in the preheated oven. Bake for 30 minutes or until the centre is firm but can be easily pierced with a fork. (You can also cook the potatoes in the air fryer at 180°C but turn them halfway through if the tops are getting brown.)

Cool the potato, cut in quarters lengthwise and cut out the centre leaving the skin with 5–10 mm of potato on it. Brush the skins with butter, sprinkle with salt and pepper and bake at 180°C for 10 minutes.

Mix ingredients for desired topping with the potato pulp and place on top of skins. Bake for another 5–10 minutes, until warmed.

Note: Use any leftover potato to make mash for salmon cakes.

Potato Frittata

Serves 4

Ingredients

1 tablespoon butter, plus extra
for greasing
1 tablespoon olive oil
½ leek, white part only,
thinly sliced
150 g button (white),
Swiss brown or oyster
mushrooms, sliced

100 g baby spinach
4 eggs
¼ cup thickened (heavy) cream
¼ cup grated parmesan cheese
1 sprig basil, chopped

Preheat the oven to 180°C and lightly grease a 14 cm cake tin.

Melt the butter with the oil in a large frying pan over medium–low heat. Add the leek and cook for 5 minutes until soft but not browned. Add the mushrooms and spinach and cook for 5 minutes.

Meanwhile, whisk together the eggs, cream and parmesan. Place the leek mixture in the prepared tin, sprinkle with basil and pour over the egg mixture. Bake for 25–30 minutes until lightly browned and set.

Cool slightly. Turn onto a board, and cut into slices or squares.

Note: You can also make the frittata in an air fryer if you have a tin that fits. Check to see if the frittata is golden and set after 15–20 minutes as the cooking time will vary depending on your air fryer.

Octopus Marinated in Oil and Herbs

Serves 4

Ingredients

⅓ cup olive oil
grated zest of 1 lemon
2 tablespoons lemon juice
⅓ cup long green shallots
  (scallions), finely sliced

2 teaspoons chopped fresh
  oregano
salt and freshly ground
  black pepper
500 g octopus, cleaned
salad leaves, for serving

In a bowl, mix together the olive oil, lemon zest, lemon juice, shallots, oregano, salt and pepper. Add the octopus, and leave to marinate for 1 hour.

Heat a chargrill pan (or barbecue hotplate over high heat) and lightly oil. Add the octopus, and cook, basting with marinade, for 2–3 minutes, or until tender.

Serve on a bed of salad leaves.

San Choy Pork

Serves 4

Ingredients

1 cup basmati rice
1 small iceberg lettuce
2 tablespoons oil
1 clove garlic, crushed
300 g minced pork
100 g shiitake mushrooms,
  finely chopped
¼ green capsicum (bell pepper),
  finely sliced

1 tablespoon mirin
2 teaspoons soy sauce
1 tablespoon oyster sauce
1 teaspoon sugar
3 long green shallots (scallions),
  chopped
1 cup bean sprouts

Place the rice in a saucepan with 2 cups of water. Bring to the boil, reduce heat to low, cover and cook for 15 minutes. Remove pan from heat, allow to stand, covered, for 10 minutes.

Carefully remove individual leaves from the lettuce, avoiding tearing the leaves. Trim with scissors to make an even rounded cup (not essential).

Heat the oil in a heavy-based frying pan, add the garlic and pork and stir-fry over high heat for 1–2 minutes. Add the mushrooms and capsicum and cook for a further 1–2 minutes.

Add the cooked rice, mirin, soy sauce, oyster sauce and sugar and toss through to combine.

Stir in the shallots and bean sprouts, remove from heat and spoon into lettuce cups to serve.

Note: Add some chilli if you want a bit of heat.

Japanese Beef with Horseradish

Serves 4

Ingredients

4 rump steaks, about 175 g each

4 tablespoons teriyaki
   or soy sauce

4 tablespoons olive oil

6 tablespoons crème fraîche

4 teaspoons horseradish cream

2 teaspoons peanut oil

7 long green shallots (scallions),
   finely sliced, plus 1 shallot,
   shredded

2 cloves garlic, chopped

¼ teaspoon chilli flakes

Place the steak in a non-metallic dish. Pour over the teriyaki or soy sauce and olive oil and turn the steaks to coat. Cover and marinate for 1–2 hours in the refrigerator. Mix the crème fraîche and horseradish in a small bowl, then cover and refrigerate.

Lightly oil a ridged cast-iron grill pan and place over a medium-high heat. Alternatively, you can cook the meat on the BBQ. Reserve the marinade. Cook for 3 minutes on each side or until cooked to your liking. Remove and keep warm.

Put the sliced shallots, garlic, chilli and reserved marinade into a small saucepan and heat through. Spoon over the steaks and top with a dollop of the horseradish cream and shredded spring onion.

Note: Serve with Asian-style salad or thinly slice and serve with steamed rice.

Any Mince Lettuce Cups

Serves 2–4

Ingredients

olive oil or vegetable oil
1 teaspoon crushed garlic
1 onion, finely chopped
500 g of whichever mince you
    prefer – pork, chicken, beef
    or turkey
pinch of salt and pepper

iceberg lettuce head or
    cos lettuce for cups
sauce of your choice to flavour
    the mince (oyster sauce,
    soy sauce)
cashew nuts or almond flakes

Heat a frying pan or wok over medium heat. Add the oil and move it around to coat the entire pan then add the garlic (make sure you don't overcook it). Once the garlic is golden and you can smell it, add the onion and cook through for a couple of minutes. Add the mince and stir it all together, moving around in the pan. Season with salt and pepper.

While cooking, wash your lettuce leaves and dry them with paper towel. Make sure each leaf is big enough to hold the mince.

After a few minutes the mince will start to look cooked through and you can add your choice of sauces to flavour the mince. Or you can use a sauce as a side dish for you to dip the cups into when the mince is cooked through.

If you like, add some cashew nuts or almond flakes into the mince as it is still cooking to add some crunch, and continue to stir through.

Once completely cooked, transfer the mince to a large bowl and spoon some mince into each lettuce cup.

You can add just about anything you want to the lettuce cups – tuna, salmon, avocado – whatever you have on hand.

Sizzling Beef

Serves 4

Ingredients

500 g rump steak
2 tablespoons soy sauce
2 tablespoons rice wine or sherry
1½ tablespoons cornflour
1 teaspoon sugar
3 tablespoons peanut oil
150 g broccoli, cut into florets

1 large red capsicum (bell
  pepper), cut into thin strips
2 cloves garlic, crushed
3 tablespoons oyster sauce
200 g bean sprouts
salt and black pepper

Trim steak of any excess fat and cut into thin strips. Put the steak, soy sauce, rice wine or sherry, cornflour and sugar into a non-metallic bowl and mix thoroughly.

Heat 1 tablespoon of the oil in a wok or large heavy-based frying pan, add one-third of the beef mixture and stir-fry over a high heat for 2–3 minutes, until browned. Remove and cook the remaining beef in two more batches, adding a little more oil if necessary.

Heat the remaining oil in the wok, then add the broccoli and 6 tablespoons of water. Stir-fry for 5 minutes, then add the capsicum and garlic and stir-fry for a further 2–3 minutes, until the broccoli is tender but still firm to the bite.

Stir in the oyster sauce, return the beef to the wok and add the bean sprouts. Toss over a high heat for 2 minutes or until the beef is piping hot and the bean sprouts have softened slightly, then season.

If you have one, serve on a sizzling hot plate to impress, with steamed rice.

Note: Before you start cooking, make sure all your ingredients are cut into pieces of roughly the same shape and size so that they cook evenly.

Veal with Lemon Pepper Mushrooms

Serves 4

Ingredients

4 butterfly veal steaks or thin veal steaks, about 150 g each

1 ½ tablespoons lemon pepper seasoning

⅓ cup olive oil

250 g flat mushrooms, sliced

1 cup thickened cream

8 sprigs thyme, leaves removed and stalks discarded

Coat the veal steaks lightly with 1 tablespoon lemon pepper seasoning.

Heat 2 tablespoons olive oil in a large frying pan over medium heat. Cook the steaks in two batches for 1–2 minutes on each side. Remove and keep warm.

Heat the remaining oil and cook the mushrooms for 2–3 minutes. Add the cream, thyme and remaining lemon pepper seasoning. Cook for a further 1–2 minutes or until the mushrooms are cooked.

Serve the veal steaks topped with mushroom sauce.

Lemon Pepper Crumbed Lamb Cutlets

Serves 4

Ingredients

8 large lamb cutlets
1 tablespoon lemon pepper
  seasoning

2 eggs, lightly beaten
1 cup dry breadcrumbs
$\frac{1}{4}$ cup vegetable oil

Sweet Potato Mash

750 g sweet potato,
  peeled and chopped
2 tablespoons butter

salt and freshly ground
  black pepper

To make the sweet potato mash, place the sweet potato in a saucepan of water. Bring to the boil and simmer for 15–20 minutes or until tender. Drain and mash. Add the butter and season to taste.

Meanwhile, trim the lamb cutlets and pound with a meat mallet to flatten. Coat lightly with lemon pepper seasoning, dip in egg and coat with breadcrumbs.

Heat the oil in a large frying pan. Add the cutlets in batches and cook for 2–3 minutes on each side or until cooked to your liking. Serve the lamb cutlets with sweet potato mash and green vegetables.

Shepherd's Pie

Serves 4

Ingredients

500 g minced lamb
750 g potatoes, peeled
   and cut into chunks
1 teaspoon salt
2 tablespoons vegetable oil
1 medium onion,
   peeled and chopped
1 stick celery, diced

1 medium carrot,
   peeled and diced
1 tablespoon tomato paste
2 tablespoons Worcestershire
   sauce
¾ cup lamb stock
salt and black pepper
25 g butter
¼ cup milk

Remove lamb from refrigerator and bring to room temperature.
Put the potatoes into a saucepan, cover with cold water and add the
salt. Boil for 20 minutes or until tender.

Meanwhile, preheat the oven to 200°C. Heat the oil in a large
heavy-based frying pan over a medium heat, then fry the onion,
celery and carrot for 2–3 minutes, until softened.

Add the minced lamb to the pan, breaking it up with a wooden
spoon. Cook for 5 minutes or until browned, stirring all the time.
Stir in the tomato paste and Worcestershire sauce, mixing well.
Cook for 2 minutes. Add the stock, stir, season to taste with salt and
black pepper, then simmer for 5 minutes.

Meanwhile, drain the potatoes and return them to the pan. Add the
butter and milk, then mash until smooth.

Spoon the mince mixture into a deep ovenproof dish, about
15 x 25 cm in size. Top with the mashed potatoes, spreading them
evenly and fluffing up the surface with a fork. Cook for 20 minutes
or until the top is golden brown.

Bacon, Onion and Potato Cake

Serves 4

750 g potatoes, peeled
and coarsely grated
1 tablespoon butter
2 tablespoons vegetable oil
1 onion, chopped
6 rashers rindless bacon,
cut into 1 cm strips

1 medium egg, beaten
1 tablespoon plain flour
2 tablespoons freshly chopped
parsley
freshly ground black pepper

Place the grated potatoes in a clean tea towel and squeeze out any excess liquid. Heat the butter and 1 tablespoon of the oil in a non-stick frying pan. Add the onion and bacon and cook for 5–8 minutes, until the onion has softened and the bacon is cooked through. Clean the pan.

Place the potatoes in a large bowl. Stir in the onion and bacon mixture with the egg, flour, parsley and seasoning. Heat a little oil in the frying pan, add the potato mixture and press into a flat round with a wooden spoon. Cook over a low heat for 10 minutes or until the base is golden.

Carefully slide the potato cake onto a large plate. Place another large plate over the top and flip the cake so that the uncooked side is underneath. Heat a little more oil in the pan, then carefully slide the cake back into the pan, uncooked-side down. Cook over a low heat for 10 minutes or until the base is crisp and golden.

Note: Great for late lunch or early dinner. Serve with a mixed salad.

Tandoori Chicken Pieces

Serves 4

Ingredients

6 chicken pieces, skin off
salt
1 cup natural yoghurt
tandoori paste, to taste
1 tablespoon butter, melted

To Serve

1 packet flatbread
crisp lettuce leaves
1 lemon

Prick the meat all over with a skewer. Sprinkle lightly with salt.

Mix the yoghurt with 4 tablespoons of the tandoori paste, adding more to taste if desired.

Rub the mixture all over the chicken pieces. Place into a non-metallic dish, cover and marinate in the fridge for 6 hours or overnight.

Place the chicken on a greased baking tray. Pour the excess marinade from the dish into a bowl. Stir the butter into the marinade.

Prepare the BBQ for indirect-heat cooking on medium heat. Set up a drip pan with a cup of water in the pan.

Place the chicken on the well-oiled grill bars over the drip pan. Cover and cook for 40 minutes or until cooked through. Brush with the reserved marinade at 10-minute intervals for first half of cooking, then at 5 minute intervals.

Place the flatbreads onto the BBQ to heat over direct heat. Remove from the grill. Cut each flatbread into 6 triangular pieces and place on a platter lined with lettuce leaves. Serve with the tandoori chicken and garnish with lemon slices.

Fried Rice

Serves 4–6

Ingredients

500 g cooked and cooled white
    rice
2 eggs
vegetable oil
250 g streaky bacon, diced
250 g prawns, cooked
    and chopped

5 mushrooms, thinly sliced
4 long green shallots (scallions),
    chopped
salt and pepper, to taste
4 teaspoons soy sauce

Beat eggs lightly in a bowl, then heat 1 teaspoon of oil in a frying pan and fry the eggs as a thin pancake or omelet. Remove from pan and slice into strips. (If you prefer, eggs can be beaten and added to the rice later.)

Cook the bacon and set aside.

Place enough oil in a large pan to cover the base and heat it. When hot, add the rice and stir fry for about 4–5 minutes or until rice is thoroughly heated through. Stir regularly, breaking up any lumps.

Add prawns, mushrooms, shallots (reserving some to garnish), and salt and pepper, then fold in egg pieces (or beaten egg) and soy sauce. Mix well. Top with bacon and remaining shallots and serve.

Note: This can be cooked on a blackstone BBQ.

Microwave Mac and Cheese

Serves 2

Ingredients

½ cup macaroni pasta
⅓ cup water
pinch of salt

⅓ cup milk
⅓ cup finely shredded firm
    cheese

Put the pasta and water in a large mug or microwave dish, add a pinch of salt and microwave for 3–4 minutes on high stirring occasionally.

Add the milk and half the cheese and stir then microwave again for another minute. Stir again until you can see it come together and then add the remaining cheese and stir until it is all blended in.

Note: You might like to add cooked diced bacon or chopped hot dog.

Herb-Crusted Veal

Serves 4

Ingredients

2 cups fresh breadcrumbs
¼ cup parsley, finely chopped
10 sage leaves, finely chopped
2 teaspoons herb and garlic salt
4 veal schnitzels or thin veal
   steaks, about 125 g each

¼ cup plain flour
2 eggs, lightly beaten
⅓ cup vegetable oil
1 lemon, cut into wedges

Combine the breadcrumbs, parsley, sage, and herb and garlic salt in a shallow dish.

Place the flour and egg in separate dishes. Lightly coat the veal in flour then dip in the egg. Lightly press the crumb mixture onto the veal.

Heat half the oil over medium heat. Cook schnitzels for 1–2 minutes on each side or until golden. Repeat with the remaining oil and veal.

Serve with wedges of lemon and roasted potatoes or a potato salad.

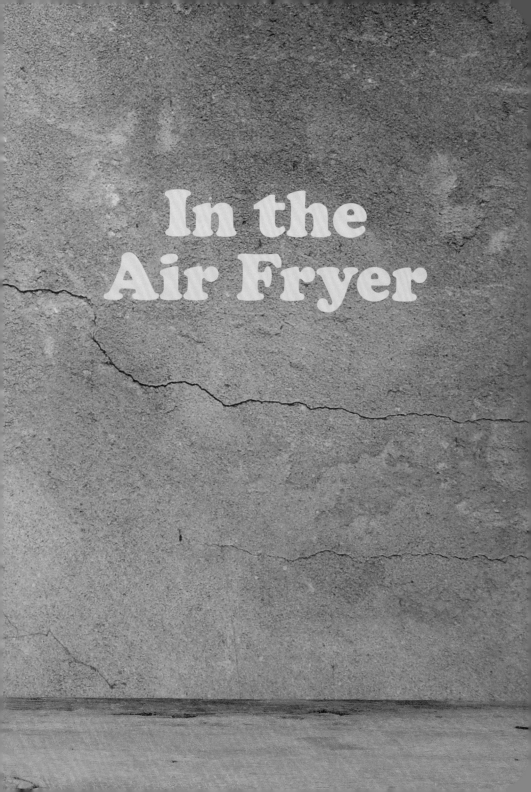

In the
Air Fryer

Corn on the Cob

Serves 4

4 large corn cobs
cooking spray or oil

salt and pepper

Spray the corn with cooking spray and season with salt and pepper.

Place the corn in the air fryer and cook at 180°C. Cook for 8–10 minutes, turning halfway through.

Note: You can make the corn Mexican style and combine salt, pepper, melted butter, chilli powder, and sour cream, brush the cobs with this mixture then sprinkle with grated cotija cheese or parmesan cheese and a little fresh minced coriander.

Wedges with Sour Cream and Sweet Chilli Sauce

Serves 4

2 large potatoes, cut into wedges
¼ teaspoon garlic powder
¼ teaspoon paprika
¼ teaspoon salt

¼ teaspoon pepper
2 tablespoons olive oil
½ cup sour cream
sweet chilli sauce

Put the garlic, paprika, salt, pepper and olive oil in a bowl or large zip-lock bag then add the wedges and toss to season.

Add the wedges to your air fryer basket and cook on 200°C for 12–15 minutes, shaking the basket every 3–4 minutes to ensure that they are evenly cooked.

Serve with sour cream and sweet chilli sauce on the side.

Note: To mix things up you could add smoked paprika for a smoky flavour, chilli powder, or grated parmesan cheese and dried parsley then toss.

Whole Roast Chicken in the Air Fryer

Serves 4

2 tablespoons olive oil
$\frac{1}{4}$ teaspoon onion powder
$\frac{1}{4}$ teaspoon garlic powder

$\frac{1}{4}$ teaspoon paprika
salt and pepper to taste
1 whole chicken

Mix the oil, onion powder, garlic powder, paprika, salt and pepper in a bowl then coat the chicken with the mixture using a brush. Reserve some of the mixture.

Place the chicken in the basket and air fry at 180°C for 30 minutes then flip and brush with the remaining spice mixture and cook for a further 20–30 minute till the internal temperature is 75˚C. Check around the 45–50 minute mark as the cooking time will depend on your air fryer.

Once done set aside for 10 minutes before serving with roast potatoes and veggies.

Salmon with Teriyaki Sauce in the Air Fryer

Serves 4

4 salmon fillets

¼ cup teriyaki sauce from a bottle, or you can make your own

½ teaspoon sesame seeds

1 long green shallot (scallion), thinly sliced or rosemary to taste

Marinate the salmon skin-side up in the teriyaki sauce for 30 minutes.

Place the salmon skin-side up in the basket and air fry at 200°C for 6–8 minutes to crisp the skin. Turn the salmon over and cook for a further 3–4 minutes or until the internal temperature is 65°C or the flesh flakes easily with a fork. Baste with teriyaki sauce once or twice while cooking.

Sprinkle with sesame seeds, shallots or rosemary and serve with steamed rice and Asian greens or steamed broccoli.

Note: You can use frozen salmon fillets; just thaw in the fridge during the day. You can also replace the salmon with chicken thighs. Just increase the cooking time to suit.

Line your air fryer basket or tray with baking paper for a quick clean up.

Baked Potatoes

Serves 4

2 tablespoons cooking oil
¼ teaspoon garlic powder

¼ teaspoon salt and pepper
4 large potatoes, skin on

Combine the oil, garlic powder, salt and pepper in a bowl.

Pierce the skin of each potato a few times with a fork or skewer or they will split when cooking in the air fryer. Rub the skin of the potatoes with the olive oil mixture.

Place in the basket and air fry at 200°C for 30–40 minutes, turning the potatoes halfway to ensure that they cook evenly.

Remove and test with a knife to ensure potatoes are cooked.

Note: This is an excellent side dish or even a meal on it own filled with cheese and sour cream or your preferred toppings.

For double-cooked potatoes cut the cooked potatoes in half and then use a spoon to carve out the potato flesh and place in a bowl. Mash with a fork or potato masher. Add some milk, butter or garlic olive oil and mix to create a mashed potato filling then add a pinch of salt and pepper. You could add cooked diced bacon and finely chopped chives to the mash.

Return the mash to the potato skin and sprinkle with cheese then return to the air fryer for another 5–6 minutes till golden brown and the cheese has melted.

Roasted Vegetables

Serves 4

2 tablespoons olive oil
½ teaspoon garlic powder
½ teaspoon onion powder
½ teaspoon paprika
salt and pepper to taste
500 g of your choice of firm
   vegetables, cut the same size
   (potatoes, parsnips, carrots,
sweet potatoes, pumpkin,
cauliflower)
300 g of your choice of soft
   vegetables cut the same as
   the firm vegetables (zucchini,
   eggplant, capsicum/
   bell pepper, mushrooms,
   tomatoes, green beans,
   broccoli)

Combine half the oil, garlic powder, onion powder, paprika, salt and pepper in a large bowl. Add the firm vegetables and toss well to coat with the mixture.

Place the vegetables in the basket and air fry at 200°C for 15–20 minutes, shaking the basket a few times to ensure that they cook evenly.

Meanwhile, mix the rest of the oil and spice in a bowl and coat the soft vegetables. Add to the air fryer and cook for a further 15–20 minutes, shaking the basket regularly to ensure that all the veggies are cooked through.

Sprinkle with mixed herbs, balsamic or parmesan cheese for additional flavour.

Air Fried Chicken Drumettes

Serves 4–6

Ingredients

¼ cup olive oil
¼ cup ketchup (tomato sauce)
2 tablespoons honey
1 tablespoon barbecue sauce
1 tablespoon Dijon mustard

3 teaspoons Worcestershire sauce
2 cloves garlic, crushed
1 kg chicken drumettes

Combine olive oil, ketchup, honey, barbecue sauce, Dijon mustard, Worcestershire sauce and garlic in a shallow dish. Add the chicken and coat well in mixture. Cover and place in the refrigerator to marinate for 2–3 hours or overnight.

Cook in the air fryer at 180°C for 20–35 minutes or until cooked.

Note: The longer you can marinate the chicken the better the flavour will be. The chicken can also be cooked on the BBQ or in the oven.

Air Fried Cauliflower

Serves 4

Ingredients

1 head of cauliflower

1 egg

1 cup plain flour

breadcrumbs

pinch of salt

Cut the cauliflower into bite-size pieces with the stalks still on.

Whisk the egg in a bowl. Place the flour in another bowl with a pinch of salt. Place the breadcrumbs in a third bowl.

Coat cauliflower in the flour first and shake off excess. Dip in the egg and then in the breadcrumbs to coat. Once all the cauliflower has been crumbed place in your air fryer and cook for 6–7 minutes on 180°C or until golden brown.

Serve with yoghurt, mayo or a dip.

You can also make this recipe with zucchini or mushrooms. Reduce the cooking time accordingly and check every few minutes as cooking times will change depending on size.

Quick
10 to 15 Minutes
in the Air Fryer Ideas

You can buy most of these frozen from the supermarket and keep on hand if you have room in your freezer:

- Spring rolls & dim sims
- Sausage rolls and pies
- Quiche
- Chicken tenders and chicken nuggets
- Chips and wedges
- Empanadas and pastry triangles
- Fish fillets, battered and crumbed fish fingers
- Sweet potato fries
- Waffles and hash browns
- Open toasted grills with cheese/ham/tomatoes
- Meatballs
- Small pizzas
- Drumsticks
- Corn on the cob
- Crab cakes
- Apple pie
- Mozzarella sticks
- Potstickers
- Garlic bread

On a Skewer

Chicken Teriyaki

Serves 4

Ingredients

2 tablespoons butter
⅓ cup teriyaki sauce or soy sauce
2.5 cm piece of ginger, chopped
2 tablespoons sugar
2 tablespoons dry sherry

500 g (2 large) boneless chicken breasts, skinned
8 long green shallots (scallions), cut into 2.5 cm strips
bamboo skewers, soaked in water for 20 minutes

Place butter, teriyaki sauce, ginger, sugar and dry sherry in a small pan over a medium heat and stir until the sugar is dissolved. Leave to cool.

Cut the chicken into 2.5 cm pieces and stir into the marinade with the shallots. Chill for at least 2 hours.

Thread the chicken and shallots onto the skewers and grill for 4–5 minutes on either side, or until cooked, brushing occasionally with marinade.

Serve with steamed rice and salad. Sprinkle with sesame seeds.

Chicken Yakitori

Makes 20 skewers

Ingredients

400 g skinless chicken breast
    fillets, sliced 5 mm thick
½ cup soy sauce
¼ cup honey

1 clove garlic, crushed
½ teaspoon ground ginger
small bamboo skewers, soaked in
    water for 20 minutes

Place the sliced chicken in a glass bowl. Mix in the soy sauce, honey, garlic and ginger. Cover and place in the fridge to marinate for several hours or overnight.

Thread one or two strips onto each skewer, using a weaving motion. Brush with the reserved marinade.

Heat grill or BBQ to high. Grease rack or plate with oil and arrange the skewers in a row. Cook for 2½ minutes on each side, brushing with marinade as they cook.

Garnish with sesame seeds if desired and serve immediately with your favourite dipping sauce.

Skirt Steak Satays

Serves 4

Ingredients

1 skirt steak, about 700 g

2 tablespoons vegetable oil

1 tablespoon lime or lemon juice

salt and pepper to taste

juice of ½ a lemon

½ cup satay sauce

1 tablespoon peanut oil

20 long satay sticks, soaked in
   water for 20 minutes

Place the skirt steak on a chopping board. Remove any membrane. With a large knife lightly score the surface in a diagonal criss-cross pattern on both sides. This has a tenderising effect as it cuts through the meat fibres; it also speeds up absorption of the marinade.

Mix the oil, lime juice, salt and pepper together. Place the steak in a flat, non-metallic dish. Pour in the oil mixture and turn the meat to coat both sides. Marinate for 2 hours, turning once. Remove from the marinade, pat dry and place on a cutting board. Slice the steak across the grain with a knife held at a 45-degree angle to the meat. The strips should be about 12 cm long, 2 cm wide and 3 mm thick.

Weave the strips onto the soaked satay sticks and gently spread them out so they are flat, not bunched up. Arrange the skewers in a non-metallic flat dish, a lasagne dish for example. Combine the lemon juice, satay sauce and peanut oil to form a marinade. Pour over the skewers. Marinate for 30 minutes.

Prepare the BBQ for direct-heat cooking on high heat. Oil the grill bars well. Slip a double foil band under the exposed part of the skewers to protect them from burning. Arrange the satays and cook for 1–2 minutes per side. Serve immediately.

Mozzarella and Tomato Skewers

Serves 4–6

Ingredients

1 small bunch of fresh basil
100 ml olive oil
salt and freshly ground
  black pepper

20 cherry tomatoes, halved
20 mozzarella balls
small bamboo skewers

Whizz the basil, olive oil, salt and pepper in a blender or bullet blender until smooth. A stick blender or mortar and pestle will also work.

Thread the tomatoes and mozzarella balls on the skewers.

Serve on a plate drizzled with the basil sauce.

Lamb Koftas

Serves 4

Ingredients

250 g lean minced lamb
½ brown onion, finely diced
2 tablespoons couscous
2 sprigs mint, finely chopped
1 sprig parsley, finely chopped
2 teaspoons ground cumin

1 teaspoon ground coriander
1 tablespoon olive oil
pita bread and plain (natural)
    yoghurt, to serve
bamboo skewers, soaked in
    water for 20 minutes

Combine all the ingredients in a bowl and mix together well with your hands.

Divide the lamb mixture into heaped tablespoonfuls. Use wet hands to shape each portion into a sausage. Thread each kofta onto a skewer and place on a baking tray in a single layer. Cover and refrigerate for 1 hour or until firm.

Cook the koftas on a preheated BBQ grill or chargrill for 8–10 minutes, or until just cooked through. Turn and brush with olive oil occasionally.

Serve with pita bread and yoghurt.

Meatball Skewers

Serves 4–6

oil, for cooking
1 onion, finely diced
500 g beef mince
1 egg
2 bacon rashers, finely diced
2 tablespoons barbecue sauce
2 tablespoons Worcestershire
  sauce
1 garlic clove, crushed
⅓ cup fine breadcrumbs
salt and black pepper, to season
bamboo skewers, soaked in
  water for 20 minutes

Heat some oil in a frying pan over medium heat. Add the bacon and the onion then cook until the onion is soft and golden.

Combine the remaining ingredients, ensuring they are well mixed, then roll into golf-size balls.

Place four balls on each skewer. Place the skewers on a medium-high BBQ flat plate and cook for 8–12 minutes or until golden brown, turning every few minutes to brown all sides.

Serve with salad and coleslaw or place the meatballs on a long bread roll.

Chorizo & Bocconcini Skewers

Makes 12

Ingredients

1 large chorizo sausage
12 small basil leaves
12 small bocconcini cheese balls
6 cherry tomatoes, halved
    or whole depending on
what you like (one piece
    of tomato per skewer)
finely ground black pepper
12 small bamboo skewers

Slice the chorizo into 12 pieces and pan fry or grill on the BBQ for 2–4 minutes or until cooked and the edges are starting to crisp. Set aside on paper towel to cool slightly.

Thread a basil leaf onto a skewer, then a bocconcini ball, a tomato half then a slice of chorizo finished with a sprinkle of pepper to taste.

Barbecue Teriyaki Tuna Skewers

Serves 4

Ingredients

4 tuna steaks,
   cut into 3 cm cubes
sweet coleslaw, to serve if desired

small bamboo skewers, soaked in
   water for 20 minutes

Marinade

⅓ cup olive oil
1 teaspoon chilli flakes
1 teaspoon brown sugar

juice and zest of 1 lime or lemon
   (whichever you prefer)
¼ teaspoon black pepper

To make the marinade, combine all of the ingredients.

Marinate the tuna in the marinade for 10 minutes.

Thread the tuna onto the skewers. Preheat the BBQ grill to a medium-high heat. Place the skewers on the grill and baste with the leftover marinade to keep moist. Cook until done to your liking, turning every couple of minutes.

Serve with coleslaw.

Prawn and Chorizo Skewers

Serves 2

1 kg green prawns,
   peeled, tails on
3 chorizo sausages,
   cut into 1 cm pieces
1 lemon, to serve

coriander (cilantro), to garnish
metal or bamboo skewers
   (soaked in water for 20
   minutes)

Prawn Marinade

1 red chilli, finely sliced
1 garlic clove, crushed
3 tablespoons olive oil

juice of 1 lemon
$\frac{1}{4}$ teaspoon salt
$\frac{1}{2}$ tablespoon ground pepper

To make the prawn marinade, combine all of the ingredients.

Marinate the prawns for 10 minutes.

Thread the prawns and chorizo alternately on the skewers.

Preheat the BBQ grill to a medium-high heat and cook the skewers for 2–3 minutes on each side.

Squeeze the lemon over the skewers then garnish with coriander and serve warm.

Vegetable & Haloumi Skewers

Serves 4

2 large zucchini
250 g baby tomatoes
300 g haloumi
250 g white cup mushroom
1 large red capsicum (bell pepper)

1 large red onion
12 baby potatoes halved
metal or bamboo skewers (soaked in water for 20 minutes)

Marinade

½ teaspoon dried rosemary
2 cloves garlic, finely chopped
pinch sea salt

½ lemon, juiced
50 ml olive oil

To make the marinade, whisk together all the ingredients.

Cut all the vegetables and haloumi to around the same size so they cook evenly. You will need to par cook the potatoes in boiling water for around 6–8 minutes.

Thread the vegetables and haloumi onto skewers in any order. You should have about 8 large skewers. Place the skewers on a hot BBQ grill or flat plate and baste with the marinade. Cook for 8–10 minutes turning several times.

Serve with a garlic aioli, pesto or a squeeze of lemon.

Lollypop Chicken Sticks

Serves 4

Ingredients

500 g ground chicken meat
½ cup breadcrumbs
1 medium onion, peeled
½ teaspoon salt
2 tablespoons chopped
    fresh parsley

½ teaspoon pepper
2 tablespoons lemon juice
oil for greasing
20 mini bamboo skewers,
    soaked in water for
    20 minutes

Place the chicken in a bowl. Add the breadcrumbs. Using the fine side of a grater, grate the onion over the breadcrumbs to catch the juice. Add all remaining ingredients except the oil. Mix and knead well with your hands to combine and make the chicken mix fine. Allow to stand for 15 minutes.

With wet hands take a portion of chicken and mould around the stick to a 3.5 cm length. Arrange on an oiled tray, cover and refrigerate for 1 hour.

Prepare the BBQ for medium–hot direct-heat cooking. Oil the grill and place the chicken sticks on it. Cook for 10–12 minutes, or until cooked through, turning frequently. Serve hot.

Indonesian Lamb Satay Skewers

Serves 4

Ingredients

500 g lamb fillets or backstraps
2 tablespoons kecap manis
1/4 teaspoon freshly ground
    black pepper
1 teaspoon Malaysian curry
    powder
juice of 1 lime

1/4 cup peanut oil
1/4 cup peanuts
1/2 cup coriander (cilantro)
metal or bamboo skewers
    (soaked in water for
    20 minutes)

Sauce

3 tablespoons butter
1 red chilli, finely chopped
3 long green shallots (scallions),
    chopped

1 clove garlic, crushed
2/3 cup crunchy peanut butter
2 teaspoons brown sugar
2 tablespoons kecap manis

Cut the lamb into large strips. In a large dish, combine the kecap manis, pepper, curry powder, lime juice, oil and 1 tablespoon hot water. Add the lamb and marinate for half an hour.

To make the satay sauce, heat the butter in a saucepan and fry the chilli, shallots and garlic until soft. Add all other sauce ingredients and 1 cup water and cook for a further 5 minutes. Pour into a serving bowl.

Skewer lamb and cook on a hot grill, turning frequently until lamb is cooked, approximately 8 minutes. Brush with marinade several times during cooking. Top with sauce, peanuts and coriander and serve with rice.

Grilled Trout Skewers

Serves 4

Ingredients

2 whole trout

4 tablespoons olive oil

2 tablespoons Cajun spice

2 lemons

bunch of fresh dill or parsley

long bamboo skewers (soaked in water for 20 minutes), plus small skewers to seal the fish

Clean and gut the fish. Cut off the fins and trim the tail with a pair of kitchen scissors. In a small bowl mix together the olive oil and Cajun spice. Slice the lemons. Wash the herbs and trim off the stalks.

Fill the fish cavity with a good handful of herbs and 2–3 slices of lemon, then pour on some of the oil and spice mix. With 2–3 small wooden skewers, fasten together the fish so the herbs and lemon do not fall out during cooking.

Turn the fish over and rub the oil and spice mix into the fish well.

Prepare the BBQ for direct-heat cooking. Oil the grill bars well. Cook the fish on each side for 8–10 minutes. Serve with mixed salad.

Note: If you can't get trout, use snapper or your favourite fish.

Fish Kebabs

Serves 4

800 g fish, cubed

bamboo skewers (soaked in water for 20 minutes)

Marinade

2 cloves garlic, finely chopped
1 small red chilli, finely chopped
pinch sea salt

½ lemon, juiced
1 cup olive oil

Thread fish cubes onto skewers.

Combine all marinade ingredients.

Place kebabs in a baking dish and cover with marinade. Refrigerate, turning occasionally, for 15 minutes.

Heat BBQ to medium-high. Cook on a BBQ plate or in a baking dish or grill for approximately 10–15 minutes depending on the type of fish you use, until fish is cooked.

Teriyaki Pork Skewers

Serves 4

Ingredients

1½ kg boneless shoulder of pork
1 cup teriyaki sauce
350 g potatoes, peeled and cut
1 teaspoon freshly chopped chilli

4 teaspoons butter
1½ cups Greek-style yoghurt
8–10 bamboo skewers (soaked
 in water for 20 minutes)

Cut the pork into 2.5 cm cubes. Place the cubes in a bowl and pour over the sauce to coat well, but keep a little to brush with while cooking. Cover and marinate in the fridge for 1–2 hours or overnight to tenderise.

Cook the potatoes in boiling salted water. Drain well and mash.

Add the chilli and butter and mix. Add extra butter if needed to make a fluffy mash.

Prepare the BBQ for direct-heat cooking and heat to hot. Turn a gas BBQ down to medium-hot when food is placed on it. Set the pot of mash at the cooler side to reheat.

Place the pork skewers on the grill. Cook, turning and brushing with extra sauce for 12–15 minutes or until cooked to your liking. To serve, pile mash in the centre of individual plates and top with the skewers. Drizzle yoghurt over the pork and season liberally with cracked pepper. Serve with a salad.

Salads and Dressings

Thai Beef Salad

Serves 4

Ingredients

500 g rump steak
2 teaspoons Thai seasoning
1 tablespoon peanut oil
1 cucumber, halved, deseeded
   and sliced
1 carrot, peeled and grated
6 long green shallots (scallions),
   sliced

1 small red chilli, deseeded and
   finely chopped
2 cups bean sprouts, trimmed
1 cup snowpea sprouts, trimmed
1/4 cup fresh mint leaves,
   chopped
1/4 cup fresh coriander (cilantro)
   leaves, chopped

Asian Dressing

1 tablespoon fish sauce
2 tablespoons lime juice
1 tablespoon sweet chilli sauce

1 teaspoon sesame oil
1 teaspoon soy sauce

Dust the steak in Thai seasoning. Heat the oil in a frying pan or
chargrill BBQ hot plate. Cook the steak for 3 minutes on each side,
or to your liking. Remove and set aside.

Cut the steak into thin slices. Place in a serving bowl with the
cucumber, carrot, shallots, chilli, bean sprouts, snowpea sprouts,
mint and coriander leaves.

Combine the ingredients for the dressing in a bowl and whisk
together. Pour the dressing over the salad, toss to combine and
serve.

Greek Salad

Serves 2–4

Ingredients

2 Lebanese cucumbers, sliced
4 Roma tomatoes, quartered
2 red onions, quartered
  and separated
75 g feta, crumbled
  or cut into cubes
½ cup whole Kalamata olives

3 tablespoons extra virgin
  olive oil
2 tablespoons vinegar
pinch of sea salt
freshly ground pepper
¼ cup oregano leaves

Place the cucumber, tomatoes, onion, feta and olives in a bowl.

Combine the olive oil and vinegar in a separate bowl, and whisk.
Pour over the salad, then season with salt and pepper.

Garnish with oregano leaves. Serve salad on its own, or with
fresh bread.

Chicken & Avocado Salad

Serves 4

Ingredients

3 skinless chicken breasts, cooked and sliced, or precooked BBQ chicken
1 small head of romaine lettuce, shredded
1 large red onion, thinly sliced

½ cup extra-virgin olive oil
¼ cup red wine vinegar
salt and freshly ground black pepper
2 avocados, peeled and sliced

Place lettuce, and onion on a serving plate.

Thoroughly combine oil and vinegar, and season to taste with salt and pepper.

Top the salad with the chicken and avocado then pour over the dressing.

Toss gently before serving.

Chicken Caesar Salad

Serves 4

2 cloves garlic, minced
6 tablespoons extra-virgin
  olive oil
9 anchovies
juice of 1½ lemons
½ teaspoon Worcestershire
  sauce
½ teaspoon mustard
2 tablespoons white wine vinegar

4 eggs, boiled for 1 minute
2 thick slices country bread
salt and freshly ground
  black pepper
125 g prosciutto
3 heads of romaine lettuce
cooked chicken breasts
  or BBQ chicken, sliced
2 tablespoons parmesan, shaved

Preheat the oven to 220°C.

Place the minced garlic and 4 tablespoons olive oil in a large bowl, and, using the base of a metal spoon, mash the garlic into the oil. Add the anchovies and mash these into the oil mixture as well. Whisk in the lemon juice, Worcestershire sauce, mustard, and white wine vinegar, mixing thoroughly to incorporate each ingredient before the next is added.

Crack the eggs carefully after they have been boiled for 1 minute, discard the whites, and add the yolks to the mixing bowl. Mix these in thoroughly, incorporating them into the other ingredients. Season to taste with salt. Set aside.

Cut the bread into cubes and toss with the remaining olive oil and salt and pepper. Transfer to a baking sheet and bake the cubes until golden, about 15 minutes. Cool.

Crisp the prosciutto in a frying pan, then break into smaller pieces.

Place the well-washed lettuce leaves in a mixing bowl and toss them thoroughly in the dressing for several minutes until all the leaves have been coated. Add the bread cubes, chicken and parmesan and finish with black pepper and crisp prosciutto. Serve immediately.

Salad in a Jar

Makes 2

Ingredients

½ cup mayonnaise or ranch dressing

1½ cups lettuce or rocket leaves

1 medium can corn kernels

2 tomatoes, chopped into small squares

1 small cucumber, finely sliced

1 avocado, sliced

cooked chickpeas, or nuts of your choice

2 jars with tight lids so the salad can be made in advance

Assembling your salad is very easy to do and takes minutes once you have prepared your ingredients. You can add whatever leftover ingredients you have like chicken, sliced steak, olives, grilled vegetables, cheese, spinach, croutons, nuts, boiled egg, peas, lentils, beetroot, beans … the options are endless.

To serve the salad you flip your salad jar onto a plate so what you want at the bottom of your plate, for example lettuce, should be put on the top of your jar.

Start by putting your mayo or dressing (you could also make your own) at the bottom of the jar then layer the other ingredients evenly as you prefer.

If you want your entire salad coated in dressing before serving make sure the lid is on tightly before shaking gently then tipping out onto your plate.

Note: Salad jars are great to prepare while making breakfast in the morning. You'll be on the road to your next adventure or enjoying your day knowing lunch is ready and sitting in the fridge.

Italian Tuna & Bean Salad

Serves 4

Ingredients

200 g canned tuna in oil,
  drained and oil reserved
125 rocket (arugula)
400 g canned borlotti or
  cannellini beans, drained and
  rinsed

1 small red onion, thinly sliced
2 sticks celery, thinly sliced
3 tablespoons flat-leaf parsley,
  chopped

Dressing

4 tablespoons olive oil
2 tablespoons balsamic
  or white wine vinegar

salt and freshly ground
  black pepper

To make the dressing, whisk the reserved tuna oil with the olive oil and vinegar, then season.

Put the rocket in a large bowl and flake the tuna on top then add the beans, red onion, celery and parsley. Spoon over the dressing and toss well to combine.

Note: The combination of colours, flavours and textures in this simple salad make it a real favourite. It's delicious served with some warmed ciabatta bread.

Moroccan Lamb Salad Wraps

Serves 4

Ingredients

500 g lean lamb cut from 6–8 lamb chump chops or a lamb back strap cut into strips
2 teaspoons Moroccan seasoning
2 tablespoons olive oil
mixed salad leaves with extra rocket (arugula)
¼ cup mint leaves, chopped
3 tomatoes, sliced
1 Lebanese cucumber, thinly slice
1 Spanish onion, sliced
1 red capsicum (bell pepper), thinly sliced
juice of 2 lemons
1 tablespoon olive oil
salt and freshly ground black pepper
8 flat breads

Sprinkle the sliced lamb with Moroccan seasoning. Heat the oil in a large frying pan over medium heat and fry the lamb for a few minutes. Be careful not to overcook.

Combine the salad ingredients (except the lemon juice and olive oil). Mix the lemon juice and extra olive oil together and season to taste. Pour the dressing over the salad.

Put a generous amount of the salad mixture into each flat bread and top with the lamb. Serve immediately.

Note: The wraps are great with tzatziki, hummus, garlic mayo or even a bit of hot sauce.

Baby Octopus Salad

Serves 4

Ingredients

1 kg baby octopus
2 teaspoons coriander seeds, toasted
2 cloves garlic, finely minced, plus 12 cloves, sliced
2 tablespoons lemon juice
¼ cup sweet chilli sauce
2 cucumbers, peeled
1 large red capsicum (bell pepper)
1 bunch watercress
1 tablespoon pickled ginger
1 tablespoon black sesame seeds
1 cup coriander (cilantro) leaves
1 cup bean sprouts
1 cup vegetable oil
pinch of sea salt

Clean the octopus by peeling off the skin and removing the heads.

Grind the toasted coriander seeds in a mortar and pestle. Combine the coriander, minced garlic, lemon juice, and sweet chilli sauce in a large bowl. Add the octopus and marinate in the fridge for 2 hours.

Using a vegetable peeler, peel thin strips of cucumber. Thinly slice the capsicum lengthwise. Combine the watercress, cucumber, capsicum, pickled ginger, sesame seeds, coriander leaves and bean sprouts in a large bowl. Set aside.

Heat the oil in a heavy-based frying pan and fry the sliced garlic until golden brown and crispy. Remove and drain on a paper towel.

Strain the marinade from the octopus into a small saucepan and bring to a simmer. Set aside to cool and use as a dressing later. Heat a wok and stir-fry the octopus until cooked, approximately 3–4 minutes.

Combine the prepared salad with octopus and toss with dressing. Season to taste. Serve garnished with crispy garlic.

Yoghurt Dressing

Makes 1 cup

2 tablespoons snipped
  fresh chives
1 clove garlic, crushed
¾ cup natural yoghurt

2 tablespoons white wine
  vinegar
salt and freshly ground
  black pepper

Place chives, garlic, yoghurt and vinegar in a bowl and whisk to combine. Very versatile and great with vegetarian dishes.

Coriander Chilli Mayonnaise

Makes about ½ a cup

Ingredients

1 small fresh red chilli
1 large bunch coriander
  (cilantro)
3 tablespoons sour cream
3 tablespoons plain yoghurt

2 cloves garlic, chopped
6 mint leaves
juice and zest of 1 lime
salt and freshly ground
  black pepper

Remove and discard the seeds of the chilli and wash and dry the coriander.

Place the sour cream, yoghurt, garlic, mint, chilli, and coriander in a food processor and process until smooth (or you could use a stick blender). Add the lime juice and zest and process briefly, then add salt and pepper to taste.

Goes well with flaked cold salmon, warm boiled baby potatoes, avocado, and asparagus.

Warm Herbed Potato Salad

Serves 6–8

1⅓ kg potatoes
2 tablespoons olive
4 white onions, sliced
¼ cup dill, chopped

¼ cup chervil, chopped
¼ cup Italian parsley, chopped
zest of 1 lemon

Dressing

⅔ cup extra-virgin olive oil
⅓ cup white wine vinegar
juice of 1 lemon

3 cloves garlic
salt and freshly ground pepper

Cut the unpeeled and well washed potatoes into large chunks, place in a saucepan, and boil in salted water for 10 minutes or until tender but not soft.

In a heavy-based skillet, heat the oil and sauté the onions over a high heat until golden, about 8 minutes. Reduce the heat, cover, and cook slowly for 20 minutes to caramelise the onions.

Drain the potatoes and return to the saucepan.

In a small bowl, whisk the dressing ingredients until thickened. Pour the dressing over the hot potatoes and toss, adding the fresh herbs and lemon zest with salt and lots of pepper to taste.

Add the caramelised onions and toss thoroughly. You can also garnish the potatoes with some finely chopped red onion for a little more bite.

Insalata Caprese (Tomato and Bocconcini)

Serves 4

400 g Roma tomatoes,
   thickly sliced
250 g bocconcini/
   fresh mozzarella,
   sliced or as small balls

½ cup fresh basil leaves,
   shredded
¼ cup extra-virgin olive oil
2 tablespoons balsamic vinegar
sea salt and freshly ground
   black pepper

Arrange tomatoes, bocconcini, and basil leaves on individual plates.

Drizzle with olive oil and balsamic vinegar, and sprinkle with sea salt and freshly ground black pepper.

Serve with crusty bread.

Tzatziki

Makes 1 cup

Ingredients

⅔ cup plain Greek yoghurt
1 small cucumber, grated
1 tablespoon lemon juice

1 clove garlic, crushed
salt and black pepper
1 tablespoon mint, chopped

Combine all the ingredients in a bowl. Cover the bowl with cling wrap and refrigerate for at least 1 hour to allow the flavours to develop.

Serve with pita bread as a dip, or as a sauce to accompany meat dishes.

Blue Cheese Mayonnaise

Makes 1½ cups

¼ teaspoon dry mustard
2 egg yolks
1 cup extra-virgin olive oil
2 tablespoons lemon juice
  or white wine vinegar

salt and freshly ground black
  pepper
90 g blue cheese, crumbled

Place mustard and egg yolks in a food processor or blender and process until just combined. With machine running, gradually pour in oil and process until mixture thickens. Blend in lemon juice or vinegar and season to taste. Add the blue cheese and process to combine.

Very rich and old-fashioned, great with endives.

Real Homemade Herb Mayonnaise

Makes about 3 cups

Ingredients

1¼ cups olive oil1
¼ cups grapeseed oil
2 cups fresh herbs of your
    choice, such as Italian parsley,
    chives, basil, chervil
2 cloves garlic, peeled

2 eggs, plus 2 yolks
1 tablespoon Dijon mustard
1 tablespoon white wine vinegar
salt and freshly ground black
    pepper

Combine the olive and grape seed oils and set aside. Process the herbs and garlic until chopped and set aside.

Place the eggs and yolks in a food processor and process for 2 minutes. With machine running, add the mustard and half the vinegar, and then add the oil mixture in a thin stream. When most of the oil has been used, stop the processor and add the herb mixture, remaining vinegar and oil, and process briefly to combine.

Add salt and pepper to taste and chill until ready to use. Store in the refrigerator.

Goes with everything.

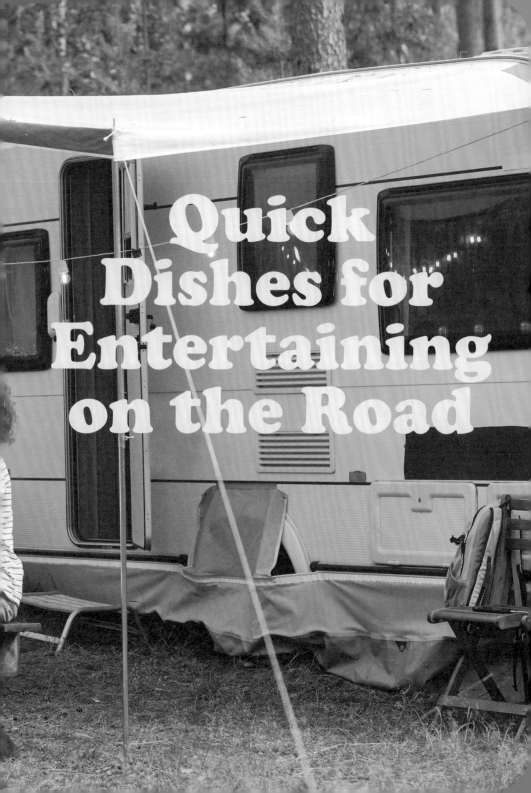

Quick Dishes for Entertaining on the Road

Quick & Easy Sour Cream and Corn Relish Dip

Ingredients

300 ml sour cream (or light sour cream if you like)
250 g jar of corn relish

bag of corn chips (chilli & lime are my go-to corn chip)

Mix together the sour cream and corn relish reserving a spoonful of sour cream to swirl on the top for decoration.

Note: Serve with carrot and celery sticks for a healthier option.

French Asparagus Dip

Ingredients

250 g cream cheese
½ packet French onion soup mix
1 tablespoon lemon juice

salt and freshly ground black pepper
310 g can asparagus, drained

Place cream cheese, soup mix, lemon juice, salt and pepper into a food processor or mix well in a bowl until combined.

Add the drained asparagus and pulse until it is roughly chopped, or roughly chop by hand then mix until well combined.

Serve with crackers.

Smoked Oyster Dip

Ingredients

125 g cream cheese

1 long green shallot (scallion),
  finely chopped

1 teaspoon lemon juice

100 g canned smoked oysters

salt and freshly ground
  black pepper

Place the cream cheese, shallots and lemon juice in a bowl and stir until smooth.

Add smoked oysters with oil, directly from the can and some salt and pepper to taste. Stir until the oysters are roughly chopped.

If you have a bullet or other blender with you, you can use it to blend all the ingredients together.

Place in a serving bowl, cover and refrigerate.

Serve with a selection of crackers or vegetables of your choice.

Smoked Salmon Dip

Ingredients

100 g smoked salmon,
   cut into strips
125 g cream cheese, cubed
1 long green shallot (scallion),
   finely chopped

2 teaspoons lemon juice
salt and freshly ground
   black pepper

Place all ingredients in a food processor and process until smooth or beat together by hand in a bowl. Refrigerate until ready to serve.

Serve with a selection of crackers.

Note: If you are making the dip without a food processor you will need to dice the salmon finer and soften the cream cheese first.

Yoghurt and Cucumber Dip

Ingredients

1 cup plain yoghurt
1 medium cucumber
1 clove garlic, crushed
1 tablespoon olive oil

1 teaspoon dill, chopped
2 teaspoons lemon juice
salt to taste

Drain yoghurt in a strainer over a bowl and set aside.

Wash and grate the cucumber and drain as above.

Combine the yoghurt, cucumber and garlic and gradually stir in the olive oil. Stir through the remaining ingredients.

Chill then serve with crackers.

Note: Makes a good dip for potato wedges as well.

Guacamole Dip

Ingredients

1 large avocado

$^1\!/_2$ cup sour cream

$^1\!/_4$ cup oil

3 tablespoons lemon juice

$^1\!/_2$ teaspoons sugar

$^1\!/_4$ teaspoons garlic salt

dash of Tabasco sauce if desired

salt to taste

You can blend all the ingredients in a food processor for a smoother dip consistency or just mix together in a bowl and mash with a fork.

Season to taste.

Serve with corn chips, crackers or vegetables.

Bruschetta

Serves 4

Ingredients

8 Roma or plum tomatoes, roughly chopped

1 medium red onion, finely chopped

10 basil leaves, chopped

salt, to taste

2 tablespoons of olive oil

2 tablespoons balsamic dressing

1 baguette

1 large clove garlic, slightly crushed

100 g butter, softened

120 g fresh mozzarella or goats cheese

In a bowl, combine the tomatoes, onion, basil, salt, oil and balsamic dressing.

Cut the baguette into diagonal slices, rub with garlic and spread with butter. Place on a hot BBQ grill and cook until golden brown.

Top the hot garlic bread with mozzarella or goats cheese and the tomato mix. The tomato mix is good if prepared a few hours in advance.

Pizza in the Air Fryer

You can use any combination of toppings you have available including deli meats, leftover vegetables and cheese to make pizza in the air fryer.

Oven or BBQ option

If using an oven cook for 15–20 minutes at 180°C on a lined baking tray.

If using a BBQ, close the lid if cooking on a Weber but keep checking the pizza as depending on the temperature it may cook quicker.

Ham and Pineapple Pizza

Serves 2

Ingredients

2 small pizza bases or tortillas
¼ cup tomato pasta sauce
2 slices ham

100 g pineapple, diced
½ cup grated cheddar cheese
½ teaspoon oregano if desired

Pre-cook the pizza base for 2 minutes and then top with tomato sauce then ham, pineapple and cheese and put it the air fryer for 7–10 minutes on 180°C.

If using a tortilla you can also choose to pre-cook the tortilla for extra crispiness but it is not necessary. Once you've added your toppings place the tortilla in the air fryer for 5–6 minutes on 180°C.

Pumpkin Pizza

Serves 2

Ingredients

½ cup tomato pasta sauce
2 very small pizza bases
   or tortillas

100 g pumpkin, diced and
   roasted
50 g feta cheese, crumbled
mint or basil leaves, to garnish

Pre-cook the pizza bases for 2 minutes and then spread the tomato sauce on top. Top with the roasted pumpkin and feta. Put it the air fryer for 7–10 minutes on 180°C. Garnish with mint or basil leaves before serving.

If using a tortilla you can also choose to pre-cook the tortilla for extra crispiness but it is not necessary. Cook in the air fryer for 5–6 minutes on 180°C.

Garlic & Cheese Pizza

Serves 2

Ingredients

2 tablespoons olive oil or truffle oil

1/2 teaspoon minced garlic

2 small pizza bases or tortillas

1/2 cup grated cheddar cheese

2 tablespoons freshly chopped parsley

salt

Pre-cook the pizza base for 2 minutes.

Combine oil and garlic and brush or spoon on your pizza base or tortilla. Season with salt. Top with cheese and parsley or whatever herbs you have available. Put in the air fryer and cook for 7–10 minutes on 180°C.

If using a tortilla you can also choose to pre-cook the tortilla for extra crispiness but it is not necessary. Cook in the air fryer for 5–6 minutes on 180°C.

Salmon Rolls with Cream Cheese

Makes approx. 20–25

Ingredients

100 g cream cheese or other soft cheese

1 tablespoon minced horseradish, if desired

8 slices of smoked salmon

freshly ground black pepper

chives, finely chopped

Combine the cream cheese and horseradish.

On a sheet of plastic wrap, slightly overlap the salmon slices. Spread with the cheese and top with a small amount of black pepper. Scatter the chives on top.

Roll up the salmon tightly in the wrap. Refrigerate, then just before serving cut into slices.

Note: Can be prepared a few days ahead of time and kept in the refrigerator, but don't cut the roll until you're ready to serve it.

BBQ Potato Wedges

Serves 4

Ingredients

4–6 medium-sized washed
    potatoes
1 teaspoon crushed garlic
4 teaspoons finely chopped
    rosemary

$\frac{1}{4}$ cup olive oil
$\frac{1}{3}$ cup lemon juice
$\frac{1}{2}$ teaspoon pepper
salt, to taste

Halve the potatoes then cut each half into 4–6 wedges. Place in a large bowl or zip-lock bag. Mix the garlic, rosemary, oil and lemon juice together, pour over potatoes and toss well to coat. Sprinkle with pepper.

Cook over direct heat in a covered BBQ for 20 minutes, turning the potatoes after 10 minutes. Cook until tender and crisp. The dish can be moved to indirect heat while other dishes finish cooking.

To serve, sprinkle lightly with salt.

Fishcakes

Serves 4

Ingredients

2 medium-size fillets of firm white fish, poached or steamed
250 g mashed potatoes
1 egg

salt and freshly ground black pepper, to taste
butter for frying
parsley and lemon, to garnish

Coating

¼ cup flour seasoned with salt and pepper

1 egg, beaten
1 cup breadcrumbs

Remove all bones and skin from the fish, then flake with a fork.

Place the fish, potato, egg and seasoning in a bowl. Mix well, and then divide into 8 round cakes.

Place the seasoned flour, beaten egg and breadcrumbs into three separate bowls. Coat the fishcakes in seasoned flour, then egg, then breadcrumbs.

Frying Pan Option

Heat some butter or oil in a frying pan and fry the fishcakes for 2–3 minutes, until golden brown. Turn, and then cook for the same time on the second side. Remove from the pan and drain on absorbent paper.

Air Fryer

Place on baking paper on a tray in the air fryer on 180°C and cook for 15 minutes or until golden brown, turning over halfway through and checking after 10–12 minutes. Serve hot, garnished with lemon.

Note: This is a good dish to make with leftover mash.

Fish Tacos

Serves 2

1 cup shredded cabbage
¼ cup sliced red onion
¼ carrot, grated
2 tablespoon sour cream
1 tablespoon mayonnaise
juice of half a lime
salt
2 tablespoon plain flour
¼ teaspoon paprika
¼ teaspoon garlic powder

¼ teaspoon onion powder
salt and pepper to taste
1 egg
½ cup panko breadcrumbs
500 g firm white-flesh fish sliced
    into 2–3 cm strips
4–6 small soft street tacos
    (tortillas)
½ lime for serving

In a bowl combine the cabbage, onion, carrot, sour cream, mayonnaise, lime juice and salt. Mix well and set aside in the fridge.

Place the flour, paprika, garlic powder, onion powder, salt and pepper in a bowl and mix well. In a separate bowl beat the egg and season with salt and pepper. Place the breadcrumbs in a third bowl. Dip the fish strips in the flour mixture then the egg and then coat in breadcrumbs.

Spray the crumbed fish strips with oil and cook in an air fryer 8–10 minutes at 180°C. Alternatively, you can shallow fry or cook them on the BBQ till golden brown and they flake easily with a fork.

To serve, top the tacos with the coleslaw and fish strips, a slice of lime and some mayonnaise.

Note: Hot sauce makes a good addition to the mayo, or even cheese, and you can add chilli powder and cayenne to the flour as well if you like a bit of spice.

Chicken Tacos

Serves 2

500 g chicken thighs
   cut into 2 cm strips
1 tablespoon olive oil
1 packet taco seasoning
4–6 small soft street tacos
   (tortillas)

1 small red onion, finely sliced
1 medium avocado, sliced
½ cup grated cheddar cheese
green leaves of your choice
cherry tomatoes, halved
squeeze of lime

Place the chicken, oil and taco seasoning in a zip-lock bag, toss until well coated and marinate for 1 hour or longer if desired.

Place the chicken strips with oil in an air fryer on 180°C and cook for 20–25 minutes, turning at the halfway mark. You could also cook the chicken on the BBQ until golden brown.

Once cooked add the chicken to your taco and finish with your favourite toppings.

Note: You could use store-bought salsa, black beans, or turn the avocado into guacamole. Make sure you add some sauces as well like coriander lime crema, salsa verde, jalapeño ranch or chilli mayo to name a few.

Nachos

Serves 2

250 g corn chips, any flavour
½ cup grated cheddar cheese
1 small red onion, finely diced
1 small tomato, diced

½ cup guacamole
¼ cup salsa
¼ cup sour cream

Place the corn chips on an ovenproof plate that will fit in your air fryer then top with cheese, onion and tomato. Cook at 180°C for 3–5 minutes or until the cheese is melted.

Garnish with the guacamole, salsa and sour cream. If you like, add your favourite hot sauce.

Quick tips to make loaded nachos

Add a protein like ground beef, shredded chicken, ground turkey, pulled pork, steak bits, bacon, chorizo, prawns or even beef chilli.

Add on more toppings like black beans, refried beans, jalapeños, shallots, corn, olives, diced pineapple, capsicum (bell pepper), and caramelised onion.

My favourite add-on is queso dip with extra jalapeños.

Fish on French Bread

Serves 6

½ teaspoon olive oil
½ teaspoon butter
1 clove garlic, crushed
½ small red onion, finely diced
500 g firm white fish fillets
    like snapper

salt and pepper to taste
¼ cup mayonnaise
1 long French bread stick
juice of one lemon

Place the olive oil and butter in a frying pan on low heat. Once the butter is melted add the garlic and diced onion and cook until softened then add the fish cook for 2–3 minutes on each side until fully cooked through.

Remove the fish from the pan and put in a bowl. Add salt and pepper and flake the fish with a fork and spoon. Once flaked add the mayonnaise and stir through until the fish is lightly coated.

Cut the French stick into circular pieces. Place on a tray and spoon the fish onto each piece of bread, adding a little more salt and pepper for taste.

Serve while the fish is warm topped with freshly squeezed lemon juice.

Tip: You can also toast your bread in the oven. Just brush a little olive oil over the bread or rub a garlic clove on each one for extra flavour before topping with the fish.

Honey and Balsamic Glazed Chorizo

Serves 2

Ingredients

1 tablespoon olive oil
3–4 chorizo sausages
1–2 cloves garlic, crushed

2 tablespoon balsamic vinegar
1 tablespoon honey

Chop the chorizo into 1–2 cm pieces. Heat the oil in a pan over medium heat and fry the chorizo until crisp and brown on both sides.

Add the garlic to the pan and cook for 2–3 minutes, being careful not to burn, then drain most of the oil from the pan.

Add the vinegar and honey and stir, coating the chorizo, and reduce till sticky, around 2–3 minutes.

Note: Serve in a dish with toothpicks or on top of crusty bread slices for a substantial snack. Great with a beer or wine.

Burrito Bowl with Chicken

Serves 4

⅓ cup panko breadcrumbs
4 chicken fillets
¼ teaspoon ground cumin
¼ teaspoon ground turmeric
½ teaspoon paprika
¼ teaspoon garlic powder
¼ teaspoon onion powder
¼ teaspoon dried oregano
1 cup cooked white
    or brown rice
juice of half a lime
¼ cup chopped coriander
    (cilantro)
½ a lettuce finely sliced

2 medium tomatoes, diced
1 medium cucumber, deseeded,
    cut in half and thinly sliced
1 large carrot,
    cut into matchsticks
½ small red onion, finely sliced
1 cup four bean mixed, drained
1 cup sweet corn, drained
1 large avocado, sliced
1 small jalapeño, deseeded
    and diced
¼ cup mayonnaise
salt and pepper

Place the breadcrumbs, cumin, turmeric, paprika, garlic, onion, oregano and some salt and pepper in a zip-lock bag and mix well. Add the chicken to the bag and press on each breast to coat in the mixture.

Remove the chicken from the bag and place in the basket of your air fryer. Spray with cooking oil and cook at 180°C for 15–20 minutes, turning halfway to ensure even cooking. Once the chicken is cooked let it rest for 5 minutes before slicing into 1 cm strips.

In a large bowl mix the rice, lime juice, half the chopped coriander and salt and pepper to taste, then set aside.

To assemble the bowls, divide the rice between the bowls then top each bowl with a sliced chicken breast. Arrange the rest of the ingredient in each bowl, top with diced jalapeños and the remaining chopped coriander, a slice of lime and a dollop of mayonnaise.

Note: Coriander lime dressing goes great with these bowls.

Sausage Crostini with Sauerkraut

Makes approx. 28

Ingredients

1 French bread stick or baguette, cut into slices
olive oil spray
4 kransky sausages
¼ cup mild English mustard

⅔ cup sauerkraut
salt and freshly ground black pepper
thyme, leaves picked to garnish

Preheat oven to 220°C or cook in an air fryer.

Place bread slices on a tray and spray with olive oil. Cook in the oven for 5–6 minutes or until just golden.

Place sausages in a saucepan, cover with water. Bring to the boil, and simmer over low heat for 5 minutes or until cooked.

Cut each sausage into thin slices. Spread the toasted bread evenly with mustard, top with a slice of sausage and garnish with sauerkraut. Season with salt and pepper then sprinkle with thyme and serve.

Note: Kransky is already hot smoked but generally needs further cooking. Boiling, baking or grilling are the most popular methods.

Salami and Cheese Squares

Makes 24

Ingredients

½ cup light cream cheese
2 teaspoons parsley,
    finely chopped
2 teaspoons chives, finely
    chopped
salt and freshly ground
    black pepper

24 pumpernickel squares
12 slices salami, halved
12 sun-dried tomatoes,
    thinly sliced
finely chopped chives

Combine cream cheese, parsley, chives and salt and pepper in a bowl and mix well.

Spread pumpernickel evenly with cream cheese mixture and top with sliced salami and sun-dried tomatoes.

Garnish with chives.

Oven-baked Onion Rings

Serves 2–4

Ingredients

2–3 large onions
¾ cup self-raising flour
2 eggs

2 cups fine dried breadcrumbs
1 teaspoon Cajun seasoning
olive oil cooking spray

Peel and slice the onions 1 cm wide. Separate the rings, removing the very small rings from the centre of the onion. You can freeze these for another time or use in another dish. Put the larger rings in a bowl of cold water.

Pour the flour into a shallow dish. Break the eggs into another dish and lightly beat. Mix the breadcrumbs and Cajun seasoning in a bowl. Remove the onion rings, one at a time and drain on some paper towel. Coat each ring in flour, dip the ring in the egg, then coat in the breadcrumb mix, shaking off any excess crumbs.

In the Oven

Preheat the oven to 225°C. Line two large baking trays with baking parchment/paper. Grease the paper with some olive oil spray.

Place the crumbed rings on the baking trays. Spray the onion rings with oil and bake for 16–20 minutes, turning over after 8 minutes so each side can get golden brown and crispy.

Once cooked, remove from the oven and place all the onions in a large bowl and salt to taste.

In the Air Fryer

Place onion rings either on a tray in the air fryer or on parchment/baking paper and cook at a chip setting of 160°C for 5 minutes and then turn over once and cook the final few minutes until golden brown.

Bacon-wrapped Prawns

Makes 24

Ingredients

¼ bunch fresh oregano, chopped
2 cloves garlic, crushed
½ cup olive oil
2 tablespoons white wine vinegar

24 large uncooked prawns, shelled and de-veined, with tails left intact
8 rashers bacon, rind removed

To make the herb marinade, place the oregano, garlic, oil and vinegar in a bowl and whisk to combine. Add the prawns and toss to coat. Cover and refrigerate for at least 1 hour or overnight.

When ready to cook drain the prawns. Cut each bacon rasher into three pieces, wrap a piece of bacon around each prawn and secure with a wooden toothpick or cocktail stick.

Cook the prawns under a preheated medium grill or on the BBQ, turning occasionally and brushing with reserved marinade, for 5 minutes or until the bacon is crisp and prawns are cooked.

Ham and Cheese Croquettes

Serves 4

Ingredients

115 g unsalted butter
1 cup plain flour
1 cup milk
1 cup chicken stock
1 cup cheddar cheese, grated
1 cup ham, chopped
1 teaspoon salt
freshly ground black pepper

nutmeg
1 egg yolk
1 cup plain flour, extra
2 eggs, beaten
1½ cups breadcrumbs
peanut or vegetable oil
   for deep frying

Melt the butter in a saucepan then add the flour and cook, stirring constantly, until smooth. Add the milk and stock, bring to a boil over moderate heat then reduce heat and simmer for 4 minutes, stirring constantly.

Stir in the cheese and chopped ham. Add the salt and season to taste with freshly ground pepper and nutmeg. Cool slightly, and then stir in the egg yolk.

Spread the mixture in a square dish, cover and refrigerate until firm, about 4 hours. Divide the mixture into squares, dredge in flour, shake off excess and dip in beaten eggs. Finally, coat with breadcrumbs.

Deep-fry the croquettes in hot oil until golden. Drain on paper towel. Or place in the air fryer for 10–15 minutes until golden brown.

Prawn Cocktail

Serves 4

Ingredients

4 large lettuce leaves,
   finely shredded
slices of lemon, to garnish

250 g prawns, cooked, peeled
   and de-veined

Cocktail Sauce

3 tablespoons thick mayonnaise
1 tablespoon tomato ketchup,
   or thick tomato puree, or
   skinned fresh sieved tomatoes

1 tablespoon Worcestershire
   sauce
2 tablespoons full cream
   or evaporated milk

Seasoning

pinch of celery salt
   or chopped celery

1 small onion, finely chopped
lemon juice

To make the cocktail sauce, mix all the sauce ingredients together in a bowl. Add seasoning and adjust if necessary.

This dish can be arranged in glasses or on small flat plates.

Divide the lettuce between the cocktail dishes and top with prawns, cover with sauce, and garnish with lemon slices. Serve as cold as possible.

Grilled Salmon with Garlic Lemon Butter

Serves 6

Ingredients

120 g unsalted butter

4 cloves garlic, smashed

1 teaspoon salt

¼ teaspoon black pepper

3 tablespoons fresh lemon or lime juice, plus wedges to serve

fresh dill or parsley, chopped, plus more to garnish

1 kg salmon skin on, cut into 6 fillets

Melt butter over medium heat. Smash garlic cloves with the flat of a large knife and add to butter along with salt and pepper. Cook for a couple of minutes, or until fragrant. Add lemon juice and chopped herbs then remove from heat.

Transfer half of sauce to a small bowl. Reserve and set aside remaining sauce in the pan – you will use this for serving. Arrange salmon fillets on a platter skin-side down and brush tops with half of the sauce from the bowl. Let salmon marinate in refrigerator for 15 minutes.

Preheat grill to medium-high. Brush the hot grill clean and oil the grates. Place salmon onto preheated grill, skin-side down. Cover and grill undisturbed, about 2 minutes on the first side. Carefully flip salmon over, cover and cook another 2 minutes. Flip again and brush tops with the remaining sauce. Continue grilling until salmon is flaky and cooked through (about another minute).

Remove salmon from grill and drizzle with reserved sauce.

Garnish with fresh herbs and serve with lemon or lime wedges to squeeze over salmon if desired.

Beef Carpaccio

Serves 4

Ingredients

500 g beef fillet
3 tablespoons extra-virgin
  olive oil
salt and freshly ground
  black pepper

125 g rocket (arugula)
1 tablespoon balsamic vinegar
pecorino cheese

Using a sharp knife, slice the beef into 5-mm-thick slices.

Lightly oil a sheet of baking paper and season it lightly with salt
and freshly ground black pepper. Arrange four slices of beef,
approximately 5 cm apart. Place another oiled piece of baking
paper on top, and gently pound the meat until it has spread out to
at least twice its former size. Repeat with remaining meat slices.
Refrigerate until needed.

Place the rocket in the centre of a plate and arrange the beef slices
around the rocket. Drizzle with balsamic vinegar and the remaining
olive oil. Serve, topped with shavings of pecorino cheese and more
black pepper.

Chicken Schnitzel Sliders

Makes 12

Ingredients

60 g panko breadcrumbs
salt and pepper, to taste
2 eggs
500 g chicken breast fillets,
   cut into 12 pieces to fit buns
1 tablespoon olive oil

12 slider buns of your choice
whole egg mayonnaise
   or some onion relish
baby spinach
2 tomatoes, sliced

In a shallow bowl, combine the panko breadcrumbs, salt and pepper. In another bowl, beat the eggs. Dip the chicken pieces in the beaten egg. Shake off the excess then dip into the panko breadcrumbs.

In a non-stick frying pan, heat the oil on a medium-high heat and cook the schnitzels until golden brown for 4–5 minutes each side.

Slice your buns in half and toast.

To assemble your sliders, spread mayonnaise on the bottom half of the buns, add a piece of schnitzel, some baby spinach, a slice of tomato and the top of the bun. Hold together with cocktail sticks.

Index